Modern Poetry in Tr
Series Three, Numb

Transgressions

Edited by David and Helen Constantine

MODERN POETRY IN TRANSLATION

Modern Poetry in Translation
No. 5, Series Three
© Modern Poetry in Translation 2006 and contributors
ISBN 0-9545367-5-4
ISSN 0969-3572

Printed and bound in Great Britain by Short Run Press, Exeter

Editors: David and Helen Constantine
Reviews Editor: Josephine Balmer
Administrator: Deborah de Koch

Submissions should be sent in hard copy with return postage to David
and Helen Constantine, Queen's College, Oxford, OX1 4AW, UK.
Unless agreed in advance, submissions by email will not be
considered. Translators are themselves responsible for obtaining
any necessary permissions and copyright clearance.

Founding Editors: Ted Hughes and Daniel Weissbort

Subscription Rates: (including postage)

	UK	Overseas
Single Issue	£11	£13 / US$ 24
One year subscription (2 issues, surface mail)	£22	£26 / US$ 48
Two year subscription (4 issues, surface mail)	£40	£48 / US$ 88

To subscribe please use the subscription form at the back of the
magazine. Discounts available.

To pay by credit card please visit www.mptmagazine.com

Modern Poetry in Translation is represented in UK by Central Books,
99 Wallis Road, London, E9 5LN

For orders: tel +44 (0) 845 458 9910 Fax +44 (0) 845 458 9912 or
visit www.mptmagazine.com

Contents

Reviews

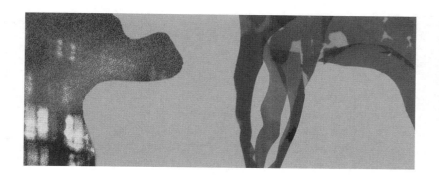

Editorial

The titles of our last three issues – 'Diaspora', 'Metamorphoses', 'Between the Languages' – have all indicated aspects or possibilities of the idea and practice of translation, whatever the subject matter of individual translations might be. The same is true of 'Transgressions'.

Translation is 'a carrying over', into something foreign and, however we strive for fidelity, always unlike. Metaphor too is a carrying over into something which is other than, and so unlike, the thing whose sense we are trying, by an act of metaphor, to bring closer and to enliven. Transgression is 'a stepping over', and from its first usage the word has always meant crossing some limit you should not cross; it has meant infringing, violating, trespassing against a law, rule or command. For translators, whatever their text, the word might allude to fidelity and infidelity; to the foreignness of the thing they are bringing in from abroad, the blatancy of its foreignness, or the homeliness and familiarity in which they disguise it. In idea and practice, all translation is more or less transgressive, whatever material it transports from one language to another.

Much of the work collected into our topic here offends, or discusses offences, against one code or another. But it is striking also how *intrinsically* transgressive many of these

translations are. W.D. Jackson, who lives in Germany, moves
from Boccaccio's Italian prose to an English verse deliberately
suggesting Chaucer and Shakespeare. Both he and Bernard
O'Donoghue move from the fourteenth into the twenty-first
century, they shift codes across, which we, as readers, might
test against our society's and our own. Pascale Petit fetches
remote and exotic myth and imagery into intimate familial
relations: transgressive strategy for survival against a lived
transgression. The German poet Dorothea Grünzweig, now
living in Finland, has acquired enough of the language of
the Mansi to put their songs into her native tongue. Derk
Wynand, born in Germany and now living in Toronto, sends
them back to Europe in his English. We have Cavafy in Scots
via French; Hsieh Ling-yün in English (the translator lives in
France) via Spanish. This issue of *MPT* is probably richer in
strange crossings-over than any before. The routes connect,
but also they estrange. We need both those effects, because
together they will quicken our interest and alertness, call us to
attend.

Transgression certainly merits our attention. When the code
itself is unjust, when it constrains and reduces life, then the
transgressor is a fighter and all too often a martyr on the side of
the angels. Laws against poems are themselves a transgression;
the makers and enforcers of those laws are the transgressors. In
their sexual relations human beings have suffered cruelly under
the codes of the great religions, especially when they aided the
code by internalizing it, so that any struggle against it was a
fight against the self, one's own mind and body, as much as
against any external authority. Guilt and self-hatred ensue, and
a hatred of the sex that arouses such bad feelings. The *frisson*
of transgression in those of Baudelaire's banned poems not
translated here, derives in large measure from a thorough
internalizing of a hateful misogynistic code. Transgression,
and the feeling of transgressing, will always be an interplay
between Law and Conscience. They may quite justly coincide;
but often they will have to fight.

Much transgression – certainly the greater part of the worst (most lethally effective) kinds of transgression – is done by legal authorities, by the state, by governments in the name of the people. This was always the case. Now the crimes are bigger and humankind and the planet can't take much more. The Mansi here can stand for many peoples and their ways of living that won't survive us and our way. And we shall sink soon after them. Native Americans watched not just with horror but also with genuine puzzlement as the incoming colonists trashed the land. Why trash what nurtures you? Trash and move on. Pastures new. Trash them.

A great deal of writing has been banned because the authorities declared it to be obscene. You could test whether a text was obscene or not by asking – as the jurors in the Lady Chatterley trial in 1960 were asked – whether 'its effect, taken as a whole, is such as to tend to deprave and corrupt'. It would be good if the governed asked themselves daily whether their government – the men and women governing them, the structures those men and women set up, their language – tended to deprave and corrupt. Power corrupts not just those in power but also those in their power. At the very least, it may make them cynical. And if you make people 'disposed to disbelieve in human sincerity or goodness', surely you corrupt them. The spectacle of government, often unedifying, is in some periods downright obscene. It has been lately, for example, quite peculiarly depraving and corrupting to listen to an Attorney General clarifying what kinds of torture are okay; or a Foreign Secretary explaining the ethical in an ethical foreign policy. Almost any sentence uttered by a President or a Prime Minister containing the words 'democracy', 'freedom', 'civilization', 'good', 'evil', 'history' or 'God' will, if we don't resist, be very likely to deprave us and corrupt us. Men in suits or uniforms telling us what a blessing cluster-bombs are or showing us with a stick how cruise missiles hit or miss their targets, are a pornography. And in a democracy, since we elected them, we are more or less complicit. Which explains the shame the governed feel when their governors act and speak so shamelessly.

There are worse blasphemies, worse obscenities, far worse transgressions than those for which in one place or another on the anguished earth you might get jailed or stoned to death. If writers can show us the real transgressors, the very big pornographers, the mouthers of the worst obscenities, and help us to resist them, they will do well.

David and Helen Constantine
March 2006

Contributions for the next issue of MPT

The next issue of *MPT*, Third Series , Number 6, will be called *After-Images*.

We are looking for translations and original poems that explore the possibilities in that title: work, for example, that is, in one sense or another, a reflection or lingering effect of somebody else's; work that has become autonomous but owes its existence in the first place to some other author. We want to cross genres too, so writing that is a response to painting, sculpture, a photograph, a piece of music, might well interest us. The earliest and strictest meaning of the word was 'the impression retained by the retina of the eye, or by any other organ of sense, of a vivid sensation, after the external cause has been removed'. Much in that definition might suggest the idea and practice of translation.

Deadline for submission to the Editors is 15 August 2006.

Submissions should be sent in hard copy with return postage to David and Helen Constantine, Queen's College, Oxford, OX1 4AW, UK. Unless agreed in advance, submissions by email will not be accepted. Translators are themselves responsible for obtaining any necessary permissions and copyright clearance.

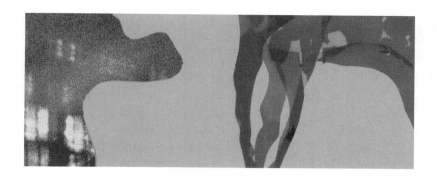

Four Mansi Songs
*Translated by Dorothea Grünzweig and
Derk Wynand*

Introduction

The songs of the Voguls, or *Mansi*, as they call themselves, part
of the Ob-Ugrian group of peoples, are highly regarded in
certain circles in Finland, where Dorothea Grünzweig has
chosen to live. Their homeland lies in Western Siberia, beyond
the Urals, along the Ob River and its tributaries.

The texts were recorded by Finnish, Hungarian and German
researchers toward the end of the nineteenth century. In the
relevant publications, they are presented without melodies,
since research on this remains undecided. But one can assume
that the melody originally had more importance than the
words, that there were primarily monotone, but also several
animated musical runs, and that the lines were for the most
part metrical, though also in free verse. The songs were
accompanied by a harp of reindeer strings, called 'goose' or
'crane' or 'singing wood'. What stands out among the Mansi is
their prayers, magic spells and bear songs.

Today some 5500 Mansi remain, but their culture suffered
most under the Soviet regime and is in the process of dying
out. Factors contributing to this regrettable turn of events are

ecocide, especially by oil companies, urban emigration, and
Putin's repressive policies concerning non-Russian peoples.
The anthropologist, Juha Pentikäinen, Finland's renowned
scholar on Ob-Ugrian cultures, refers to the current situation
as 'genocide'. There are, to be sure, signs of a counter-
movement, initiated by the Mansi themselves, but also by
scholars of different nationalities.

The Vogul language is part of the Finno-Ugrian language
group – that is, a synthetic language the textual body of
which encompasses far less space than, for example, Germanic
languages.

A distinguishing feature of the song texts is their
parallelism, using variations on a building block – as well as
doubling in epithets, such as 'his ten-toothed, toothed maw'.
Existing formulas are taken up, repeated, and modified. A
cyclical sense of time, the dependence on stable and yet mobile
structures of nature, the interwovenness of man and nature in
general, may all have played a part for this art form. The
repetition also buys time for the performer, a principle also
familiar to the oral tradition of the Finnish *Kalevala*. The
formulas are, as the researcher and translator, Raija Bartens,
says, 'elemental bits of a tribe's memory cosmos'.

The belief system of the Mansi includes a vast number of
deities and spirits like the Moosj, the forest spirits, with the
god, Torem, occupying the highest place in the heavens. The
World Surveyor, or man observing the world, is the son of the
highest god, who, after the spread of Christianity, took on
features of Christ. Birds, waterfowl especially, are established
between the invisible beings of the heavens and the creatures
on earth and beneath the ground. For Torem and the other
deities and holy beings subordinate to him, man feels awe and
humility and total dependence. He must show his reverence
with pious conduct and offerings, something that also allows
him to render them merciful.

Four Songs

Sacrificial Song

I set down a steaming bark basket
I set down a steaming bowl,
a mug of beerwater
a mug of honeywater.
Beerwater set down by me
honeywater set down by me –
accept as horned blood offering
accept as hoofed blood offering.
Take away hummockland grabbing my hand
take away pitted land grabbing my foot.
May sickness spirit not arise
may badluck spirit not arise.
Let the maw of badluck turn away
let the maw of sickness turn away.
I have no daughter for badluck spirit's mouth
I have no son for sickness spirit's mouth.
May a bright day come, so I can wander!
Golden light, golden father –
for that I weep, for that I pray.

Shaman's Invocation to the World Surveyor

Golden one, dwelling above seven on wings
golden one, dwelling above seven on foot!
Your wretches dressed in their woefur
pray to you full of woe
weep to you full of woe.
When the fog of sickness spirit rises
press the fog of sickness spirit down.
When the fog of misery spirit rises
press the fog of misery spirit down.
Here, into the hut in which seven many winged gods are
    sitting
seven many footed gods are sitting,
fall down as downcoming raindrops
fall up as upcoming winddrops.
On the girls' age leave us an age word
on the boys' age leave us an age word.

Note

The Voguls still had shamans until the eighties of the
twentieth century. They were intermediaries between human
beings and the highest god, whom even the shaman was not
permitted to see directly.

The shaman is a person who accepts solitude, isolation,
overexertion as his burden as bridge-builder, holy helper and
healer. When he falls into a trance, a sense of the synthesis of
all things flashes through his mind.

In the ritual performance of the following song, the shaman
sings the tribesmen who have come flocking in into birds, into
wild geese and wild ducks. For a long time, only men were
admitted to these most sacred occasions. Lennart Meri, the
Estonian playwright, film maker and − later − President of

Estonia, has made films about the 'Waterfowl People' as he calls them, the Ob-Ugrians.

The shaman's own voice transforms itself in this song into the voice of a goose — it has magical powers that let those gathered around believe they will be of sound limb. The shaman, accompanying himself on the *goose*, gives the song to his tribesmen. Insofar as he describes the people as geese, they are, as it were, also made to resound. A cosmic event is here depicted: The earth begins to turn. The world's out of joint. Or the earth is reborn once again. In harmony with this event, human beings are to be helped. This suggests a thought process that intertwines the fate of the individual with the whole, in this case, with 'Mother Earth'.

Shaman's Waterfowl Song

Little sons, little sons!
As gooseflock stream have you streamed
as duckflock stream have you streamed.
Little sons, little sons!
What ails you
what fails you?
Little sons, little sons!
My raincoat from the Hill-Luck-Spirit
is — behold — spread out.
My coat from the Wood-Luck-Spirit, which my mother
has stuffed with live sable
is — behold — spread out.

Little hearts, little hearts!
What ails you
what fails you?
Sing to me with a merry goosecackling voice, little sons!
I sing for you with the singing voice of
the morning cuckoo, little sons.
And when I open my rivergoose cacklemouth
overnight overday strong bones
strong flesh – behold – will rise from the earth
– behold – from the water.
We have this wish – behold – this want
we plead because of this wish – behold – this want
we need a happy day
we need hale foot, we need hale hand.

Little sons! Then when you beseech me
and once I beat my wings
the earth will go all a-tremble
when I beat my wings again
the water will go all a-tremble.
And when my Ob-water sense rises
when my sea-golden Ob-golden holy sense rises
and I wave the holy staff with its seven notches
clutched in my goodside hand
the hunched holy earth will go all a-tremble.
May my warm fur, my warm fur boots
with their bit of warmth
make your bones grow
make your flesh grow.

Note

In scholarly texts, the Mansi bear songs are described as
unique. Their particular feature is that they are set in the first
person, in a way that animal and human identities become
confused. Several researchers speak of the bear as a totem

animal for the Mansi. One reason for the high regard of the songs in Finland may be a cultural overlap, since Finland too had a bear cult.

The bear hunt, which never took place out of a need for food, but rather because of the bear's threat to man and beast, falls within a framework of rituals for the bear feast that also include bits of burlesque theatre. The bear is a sacred animal and comes from the heavens. His soul returns there. All the bear rites deal with the guilt that man heaps upon himself when he kills the bear. The bear's death is mourned, even as it is celebrated that he may now go back to his origins. The animal's sacredness as well is given expression by the fact that a taboo language was developed – the assumption was that the bear can always hear everything. In the following bear text, a condensed version of the original in three parts, the word 'bear' is actually 'animal' or 'game', one of the words of the taboo language. The closing lines, which deal with the different sums of money, either suggest that a bear who has attacked man or beast is worth less and his soul may not enter heaven. Or it points to the different worth of a male and a female creature. Thus women were not permitted to take part in important bear rituals.

The bear songs and the plays that go with them are striking a particular chord again with today's young Mansi.

The Spirit Lord's Bearkill

The highest god, father mine
created me, the shyback oathbear.
I roam the sacred sootbarked earth
where the underlings dwell.
I wade through thickest kneehigh moss.
And found a moor's sunwarm edge.
I chased after sleep, sound enough for neckchopping
I chased after sleep, sound enough for shoulderchopping.
One forepaw I used
for a pillow, tenflapped, trimmed with flaps
which my mother, the Moosj woman, had sewn.
The other forepaw I used as a cover
cut out at the neck, trimmed with swans
which my mother, the Moosj woman, had sewn.

Sleep, sound enough for neckchopping
I chased after.
One earlet of mine eavesdropped on the land
sacred land god dwelled in
heard the true oath's swearingvoice.
One eyelet of mine is overcome by seven jolts of deepsleep.
On my flankerman's flank a deepthroated
throatthunder is rumbling.
The bear's three three leaps I leap
the bear's four four leaps I hop.
I turn around
I twist
my sinewy necknape.

Look how I'm hunted by the whitehorsed man!
The white horse came to a halt at my side.
The sublime flaming sword of Torem appeared
the sacred flaming sword of Torem appeared.
A painsnouted horsefly stung
the sacred bear's little mortal spot.

And I saw:
When I, sacred bear, had my four buttons unbuttoned;
when I, sacred bear, had my fur stripped off.
Into a threeribbed birchbark cradle
am I laid,
in a fourribbed birchbark cradle
do I wake up.
Just look!
I reach the lodge door
streaming with molten gold.
The many village women arrive.
The many village men arrive.
They play watergames.
They play squirtgames.
I am carried through the lodge door
streaming with molten gold.
I may watch the girls' endless pastime.
May watch the boys' endless pastime.
When I am let go
on my way to the great god
I come into the jangling of great money
on my way to the little god
I come into the jangling of little money.

Magibearheyhey!

*German versions from the original and introductory material by
Dorothea Grünzweig translated into English by* Derk Wynand

Acknowledgements:

1. Sacrificial Song: 'I set down a steaming bark basket' (*Einen dampfenden Rindenkorb* . . .), *Wogulische Volksdichtung, Vol. I, No. 81*, edited, and with interlinear translations, by Artturi Kannisto and Matti Liimola. Published by the Finno-Ugrian Society of Helsinki, 1959.

2. Shaman's Invocation: 'Golden one, dwelling above seven on wings' (*Über den sieben geflügelten* . . .), *Wogulische Volksdichtung, Vol. V, No. 1*.

3. 'Goose' song: 'Little sons . . .' (*Söhnchen, Söhnchen*), *The Great Bear – A Thematic Anthology of Oral Poetry in the Finno-Ugrian Languages*, Finnish Literature Society, Helsinki, 1994. German text and introductory material from Dorothea Grünzweig's essay, '*Die Holde der Sprache*', ('The Holde of Language'), Ulrich Keicher Verlag, Warmbronn, 2004.

4. 'The World Surveyor's Bearkill', (from *Die Bärerlegung des Geisterfürsten*), *Wogulische Volksdichtung, Vol. IV, No. 15*.

Thanks to Prof. Ulla-Maija Kulonen of the Finno-Ugrian Society and Dr. Senni Timonen of the Finnish Literature Society for their help with the original Vogul texts.

Meles Negusse, 'Wild Animals'
Translated from Tigrinya by Charles Cantalupo

What are you running away from?
Where would you like to be?
Forget your jungle
And come to the city.

Not even one bush remains
Back there. Enough thunder
And the ground always shaking.
Here you can take it easy.

Look, the gate opens.
Leave your fear outside.
Welcome.
Young or old, women or men –
No one should be denied
The comforts of civilization.

Or has the jungle
Already seen it come,
Leaving mines instead of trees
And trading you sulphur
For the breath of freedom?
Better take the city instead

And let that wild man
Sniffing blood
Live the way you used to
But not any more —
Eating his own kind
Dead or alive.

He can have your place.
Come to the city and thrive.
Hey, tiger and deer,
Try a little peace.
Lion, lose the roar.

You can rule with justice.
Snake, you don't have to bite
The dove when you kiss.
And fox, forget the deceit
When you talk with the rabbit.

In the city we all get along.
The war of every man
Against every man belongs
In the jungle.

Leave it behind you.
Take the leap.
The change will be good.
Try my bed to sleep.

እንስሳ ዘገዳም

ንምንታይ ትሃድሙ
        ናብይ'ዩ እዚ ህድማ
ግደፍም በረኻ ንዉ ሽተማ
'ቲ ትድቅስሉ ቆጥቋጥ ተቦርቀሕቛ
ሂም ሂምታ በዚሐ ከውሒ ተጎቚኒቛ
        ንዉ'ምበር እተዉ
        ክንክፍቶ ካንሸሉ
        እንታይ ኬንኩም ትስግኡ
        እቲ ዘሉ አበይ አሉ?
ምስ ሸማግለ አረገውቲ
ምስ ቄልዓ ሰበይቲ
ክትነብሩ ምእንቲ
        እተዉ ንውሻጠ
        የለን ዋላ ሐደ።
እቲ ትነብሩሉ ብስብ ተባሒቱ
ፈዕ ትብልሉ ሜካ ቃራት ሸቲቱ
        ገረብ መሲልኩም ብረት ከይትረገጹ
        ከተማ ብሃጉ በረኻ ቅበጹ
                አብቲ ናትኩም ቦታ
                ከም መተካእታ
        ስብ አሉ፡ ስብ አራዊት፡
        ፈን ፈን ይብል ደም ይሽትት
ንዉ ቖይሩና ንሕና ክንሽፍቶ
ስብ ንስብ ከበልያ ሕሜኹም ክንብሕቶ።
        ለውጢ'ኮ ጽቡቅ'ዩ!
        እተዉ ከተማ፡ ጫለብጌዕ ሕረዱ
        ተዓረቝ ድማ ነበሪ ጫለበዱ
አንበሳ አይትግዓር ስቐ ኢልካ አመሐድር
ተመን'ውን አይትንከስ ምስ ርግቢት ሕደር
        ወኻርያ ትም በሊ
        ምስ ማንቲለ አዕልሊ
        አይትመናጨቲ
        ተሳነኹም ኪዱ።
ንሕና'ውን ክንለምዶ እቲ ናትኩም መንብር
እናተበላሳዕና በረኻ ክንሰፍር
እንስሳ ዘገዳም አብ ዓራት ደቅሱ
ስብ አራዊት ይኹን ንሽኹም ንገሱ!
ተሐዲግኩም ቦታ አይትሽቖረሩ
ከተማ እተዉ ሕጊ ተቆይሩ'ዩ!

Meles Negusse's poem will appear in:

Who Needs a Story?
Contemporary Eritrean Poetry in Tigrinya, Tigre and
Arabic

Hdri Publishers   Asmara, Eritrea, 2006
ISBN 99948-0-008-6

Charles Cantalupo and Ghirmai Negash
The first anthology of contemporary Eritrean poetry in
translation ever published, *Who Needs a Story?* features Eritrea's
most accomplished poets over roughly the last three decades.

"For at least four thousand years – from the ancient stele in
Belew Kelew to the 20th-century battlefields of Eritrea's
heroic struggle for independence – and into the 21st century,
Eritrean poets have never given up writing in their own
languages, which is why their poetry thrives. Who Needs a
Story? *translates this remarkable legacy."*
NGUGI WA THIONG'O

Hubert Moore
'Removals'

The Infinitive

to see a hair
or piece of grit that's lodged
inside the reddened lower lid
of someone's eye

who holds the lid
as wide as in your first
his third language he can
and to remove it

Too much good

Too much good men you torture.
You come my country. We talk
your very good English, my English.

Back home government say,
You good government soldier,
you find rebels, torture, kill.

You wait in car, government say,
till late night, till newspaper finish.
You kill tell-truth journalist.

You hide head low in city.
Government too much disappointed,
want kill you now, torture you.

You steal passport, come my country.
You too much good your government.
My government too much disappointed.

Removals

I think I was sorting through old recipes
when the men went to your cell.
You'd said if they tried to take you you'd refuse.

No word since so they took you: handcuffed,
in an unmarked windowless van.
During which time I must have taken my tins off

for recycling. Not that one thing ever equals
another: you being escorted
into Departures or rather Removals,

me coming home to find that my bread-alarm
has been buzzing and the crust
is baked tough already. Long-term I'm

at a loose end, I guess, undetained, untortured,
unflanked by two armed guards.
You're belted to what's being done to you, thwarted

back to the country you fled from to the fierce
heat of your choicelessness.
When your plane comes in, you said, there'll be soldiers

there to arrest you. Indeed a lorry-load of us
has just clattered into Arrivals.
I wonder if in your terror you will recognize me.

The ultimate rendition

is
to find a word
of quiet dignity, impeccably
connected (music, literature),
that will ask no questions
and will stop at nothing
(not the sending

of a man
across a sea by plane
to somewhere else so somewhere else
can torture him and we don't have to)

and will make it seem
a mild necessity, it happens,

like the sea's gesticulations,
clenching, heaving upwards
as the plane flies over,

like dread
that trickles coldly down the spine,

like handcuffing-sores, like sobs.

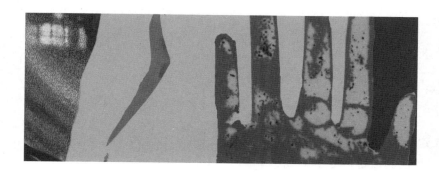

Sasha Dugdale
Lot's Wife

I put everything into a grain sack
And fled. Because we are righteous, he said

But oh, I would have preferred to be beautiful.

I took nothing but food. The children's toys
And nothing for me, although two novels

Lay trembling in the fire's heat. Take me. Choose me.
In case of fire take care, I read,

But care is the heaviest of all.

After the wind came the earthquake
And fire and then the still small voice
Brushed us along the streets and we ran

The lonely streets where the dung and decay
Would come sure as a flood and a furnace.
And women's faces will melt, he said

And he will take back the bone he once lent
He said. But the breast is now closed.

Still you are the righteous. I am not.
We have never climbed like this in our lives
The scenic spots and the coin telescopes
Are hours behind. I will do something bad

Wrung out in this way, in the wild
With the roots showing sharp
And the bags, and the nails.
I would prefer to be them.
No longer of him.

Take back the bone and throw it
So it arches and spins through the air
And is seized by wild dogs

Who sleep in the day and are kicked
Lying with their sixteen nipples exposed
In underground passes.

But in darkness and now their black lips are drawn
And their wolf teeth are white. Toss them
That bone.

The city was built on a grid and at night
From planes it appeared a luminous cage
I did not dance, it is true.

I covered my head. I threw coins
To the poor and spooned soup
Into bowls, and touched shoulders and smiled.

I washed their hands.
But I could have been sheer and cool
And worn feathers and gold
There is not much difference. I was not allowed.

What have I got within me that is righteous?
Only the love of a people on the brink
Of disaster. The kindness of those
Who will die stinking

Between paper walls.
No. I envy the ones
Who did as they chose —

You'd say depraved. As I climb
All alone and into the wilderness
With a Lord and a box of matches

And the universe expanding
Speckled with stars racing apart
Lighting me with their ancient destruction

Your mineral words dissolve
Into the ground from whence they came
And the small voice is gone.

Look at your people.
I speak for the first time. Look
At your own life.

And so I turn. I turn
And I see —

Pascale Petit
Three Poems

The Banquet

In the end, there's only one way
to stop the dead harming the living,

that's what the Guayaki Indians believe,
so they're helping me build a grill.

All week I fasted, until I too
chanted 'human fat is very sweet'.

The shaman cuts up the bodies,
separates arms and legs from trunks.

But only a daughter can shave off
her parents' hair and bury it

along with her mother's womb.
I boil my father's penis, offer it

to a pregnant woman who wants a son.
The meat roasts slowly. Fat

crackles and drips along the slats
and is sucked up by old women.

Only when all traces of blood are cooked
do we carve and hungrily eat – each mouthful

slips easily down my throat,
served with palmito buds

to weaken the force of their flesh.
I wrap the leftovers in ferns

to be eaten cold tomorrow. Every bone
will be cracked, the marrow extracted.

When the banquet is over, my friends
wash me with sap from the kymata creeper.

Self-Portrait as the King Vulture's Bride

The morning I buried you there was a thick fog
like embalming fluid. I waited and waited

at the morgue – a low red building like an open wound.
You lay in your rough coffin, ice-cold,

with that burn-bruise, and I leant over
and kissed your cheek. It was rainbow-coloured

like a king vulture's — coral-rose, storm-purple,
some white hairs pushing through

like a hatchling's first plumage
or last night's stubble. You flickered from father

to vulture, and I flickered beside you.
My flight feathers whistled as I rode the thermals

to get closer. Dear baby Dad, dear bridegroom —
see how I was the first to arrive at the carcass.

Dragon-Daughter

I drank the bile from her breast
and stored it in my body to turn to fire later —

when she made me speak, my voice trembled
and a fire-cloud escaped, burning her face.

I was a silent and sullen child, deep
as a well, magma boiling at its base.

Getting me to talk was like drawing water
and bringing up a lava-bomb.

Zhou Zan
'Scapecat'
Translated by Pascale Petit

They hung him   after a battle
between two gangs of kids.
One side was called Eight Roads   the other Japanese
    Ghosts.
The fighting broke out behind the bleachery
and village storehouse   it was May after wheat harvest
the dung heap and thresher were their bunkers.
The wounded flung themselves into bales
and would always smell hay in their nostrils.
Yet the battle always ended the same   the enemy
was beaten   and officers Matsumoto or Gumi arrested.
An old black cat was the last victim
as he happened to pass by
he was captured   they said his scream
was the enemy's death struggle,
and announced the lynching   although back then
they didn't know anything about hanging as
    punishment   or
how many war criminals and murderers   ended their lives
    by the rope.

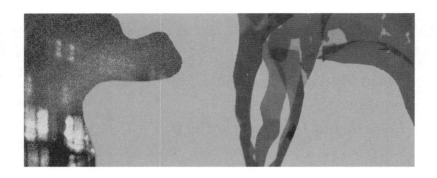

Andreas Angelakis
'Constantine in Constantinople'
Translated by John Lucas

Note

The following poem is my translation of the first of *Ten Metaphysical Nights with Cavafy*, a book-length sequence by the Greek poet, Andreas Angelakis, published in Athens in 1984. He and I began work on translating the sequence in the late 1980s but only managed to complete the first poem to anything like our joint satisfaction before he was taken ill and died in 1991. Because Andreas was gay – he was in fact Greece's first openly gay poet of modern times – he had access to idiomatic expressions that I, a non-gay, found difficult to understand, let alone translate adequately. Of these, perhaps the one that caused us most difficulty was 'very rich action', which is my literal translation of a phrase that Andreas told me means 'overt sexual activity of all kinds'. But he agreed that it was better to leave the phrase unexplained in the hope that it wouldn't confuse. I should add that each poem in the sequence begins in deliberately prosaic manner, with a rehearsal of some key facts, before moving to a more rhythmed form of utterance.

Constantine in Constantinople

Here are the facts. In 1882, because of the riots,
Constantine left Alexandria for this other city,
and he stayed there until October 1885. Then
he returned to his birthplace, together with his mother
and his two brothers, Alexander and Paul.

So much for the facts. The rest is far more difficult.
Cavafy scholars admit, reluctantly, that it must have
    been here,
in Constantinople, that he came to realise his homosexual
    nature and,
with the help of his cousin, George Psylliaris, to act on it.
Well, that's something, they could have refused to
    acknowledge
even that much, leaving it, as so often,
buried in history's catacombs. Certainly, I can
strike no sparks to light up this dark period.

Apart, that is, from the cousin. Did Cavafy
ever let fall his name, however allusively?
I must write again to Malanos, and soon,
he must, surely, have hoarded an indiscreet whisper?

Yet would it make any difference? At all events,
it's no great effort to imagine George Psylliaris,
already a man of the world, let's say, experienced,
well-built, perhaps fleshy, and with a wandering eye.
Not a *poetic* eye, none of that nonsense,
don't think of him as lithe and sentimental,
and don't confuse *him* with Constantine's sensitive heroes
trailing through seedy backwaters, among smells and
    screams,
whispering Meleager's poetry, while all around
are sag-bellied, moustachioed men, rank breath and sweat –
all to make the heart hammer – that well-known reaction.

Well now, I imagine Psylliaris soon understood
his delicate cousin's case, that virgin soul,
that adolescent who'd not yet found himself,
but who still, unwillingly, ogled elegant ladies:
a dandy, puzzled, frightened, hiding his anguish,
pretending he, too, could be the urgent bridegroom.
George sensed all that, of course, and turned it to profit!

Perhaps it was after a banquet, a drinking session.
(did Cavafy drink then – hardly. Not with his phobias,
the restraints he placed on himself. No, it's not likely
he'd risk turning loose what cost him such pains to lock up.)
Yet *raki*! That can undo the tightest knot.
Say the cousin embraced him as a relation,
or as friends do – we *are* friends, aren't we? –
then caressed his hand (as Turks will, even now,
looking that special way at their special friend),
then guiding it gently but with a definite purpose
exactly to that place, trusting his instinct.

In the dark, Constantine blushes. He protests
'you mustn't, what are you doing' – that kind of thing;
'what's the matter with you, don't', I hear him mumble.
But *raki* can break all strength and all resistance –
(resistance: come on now! who's cheating who?)
The air is heavy, the paved roads empty, no one
sees, their shirts stick to their damp bodies,
and I hope, oh how I hope, his cousin kissed him.

But I don't suppose he did. As in a thousand
other cases he used him instead of a woman,
turning his face away, brusquely unbuttoning
Constantine's clothes.
                    And that's why Constantine's
poetry is so deprived of affection,
of love – let's not avoid the word – and full
of anguish. Well, that's the way I see it.

And yet I could be wrong. Perhaps he did kiss him.
He reminded George of a girl: clear complexion,
slim body, lustrous black eyes, deep, wondering,
and also, perhaps, grateful to his cousin,
to the one who now turned fantasy to flesh,
and gave him flesh to serve, a neck to lick.

But then again a Turkish Bath* might have served.
(Needless to say, even now, in such a bath,
there's very rich action.) With soft, scented soap
rubbing each other all over, pouring water,
seated on flat stones some way from the others,
someone might have started crooning a love song,
the rest would have been busy cleaning themselves,
and the hands of the cousin, George, experienced,
go down, slowly down, rubbing his buttocks,
go slowly up the back, then down again,
then stop.
                Constantine doesn't react,
he feels as though his veins are clogged with honey,
his eyes are closed. He knows now that for years
he has been waiting to discover this himself.

But others are looking and some know what has happened.
George and Constantine dress quickly and leave.
They say nothing, it's better to let the night
lead them into this curving empty side street. Now
They embrace . . .
                And so on. Imagine the rest for yourselves.
As for the other facts, so to speak,
experiences with women that go to show
Constantine is a bisexual — what nonsense!

I hope I make myself clear, it's important I do.

*'*tsoukourtzouma hamam*'. In a letter to me which he wrote not long
before his death, the poet noted that 'this place exists in Constantinople
and is well-known in international gay culture', and he wondered
whether the phrase shouldn't be retained in my translation.

Constantine Cavafy
Two Poems
Translated into Scots, via the French,
by John Manson

The French versions, reprinted below, were first published in
La Semaine Egyptienne, 25 April 1929.

Ionian Sang

We hae smashit their eemages,
        chasit thaim out o their tempils:
they're no deid o't, the Gods.
They are luve ye dearlie, land o Ionia,
and their speerits are mind o ye.
Whan an Aagast morn comes til licht on ye,
the air's fuhll o thaim;
and whiles an ephebe's speerit,
bleerit and rapid,
makes its wey owre yir hills.

Chant Ionien

Nous avons brisé leurs statues,
nous les avons chassés de leurs temples:
ils n'en sont pas morts, les dieux.
Ils te chérissent encore, terre d'Ionie,
et leurs âmes se souviennent encore de toi.
Quand un matin d'août vient se poser
sur toi, l'air frémit de leur présence;
et parfois la forme éthérée d'un éphèbe,
indistincte et rapide,
passe sur tes collines.

Fur Theim Til Come

Ae cannle's eneuch; its waik licht's
a better suit, it'll be mair fittan
whan they'll come, frae luve, whan they'll come,
the Shedas. Ae caunle.
In the room, the nicht, nae strang licht.
A ae oo I the dwaum, and the associe,
wi a glim o licht! And sae
in the dwaum, I'll hae fantises,
fur thaim til come, frae love, fur thaim
til come, the Shedas.

Pour qu'elles viennent

Une seule bougie, c'est assez sa faible
clarté convient mieux, elle sera plus agréable
lorsqu'elles viendront, de l'amour, lorsqu'elles
viendront, les Ombres. Une seule bougie.
Dans la chambre, ce soir, pas de forte clarté.
Tout entier dans la rêverie, et la suggestion,
avec de la lumière à peine! Et dans la
rêverie, ainsi, j'aurai des visions,
pour qu'elles viennent, de l'amour, pour qu'elles
viennent, les Ombres.

Victor Manuel Mendiola
'Your Hand My Mouth'
Translated by Ruth Fainlight

Victor Manuel Mendiola was born in Mexico City in 1954 and is the author of numerous poetry books, anthologies (including *Sol de mi Antojo*, of homoerotic poetry; *El Corazon Prestado*, of poetry with pre-Columbian themes; and *Tres Caminos*, of Jewish Literature in Mexico), and books of literary criticism. In 2003 the UNAM University Press published his complete works, *Tan Oro y Ogro*. Mendiola is a member of Mexico's *Sistema Nacional de Creadores* and in 2005 he was awarded the Latino Literary Prize that is given by the Latin American Institute of Writers in New York. It is important to note that in 1981 Juan Rulfo awarded Mendiola one of Mexico's most prestigious grants. As editor and publisher, Mendiola founded the Ediciones el Tucan de Virginia poetry press twenty-six years ago, which to date has published over two hundred books of poetry by poets from all over the world. Mendiola was president of Mexico's PEN Club (under his direction the PEN centre for Cubans in exile was founded) and the Rockefeller Foundation gave Swanscythe Press a grant to publish Mendiola's poetry in the United States.

1. A plate is a hand hollowing with thirst or hunger.

2. A plate is a hand opening its depths to receive or to grasp.

3. Although its kindly aspect gives me hope, the plate – this hand – has no qualms.

4. The plate gives, shams generosity, but the knife is close behind.

5. The plate is a hard and dreadful hollow. In spite of its measured and pleasant appearance, blood and bones lie at the bottom.

6. It does not matter if I am well or badly dressed, it does not matter if I am well or badly behaved, when the plate rests before me, it overpowers me and makes me – whether I become boy or woman – the armed man.

7. A plate on the table is a moon over a ghastly wood.

8. On the hard plane
   of the wooden table
   unmoving, bleeding,
   the moon's plate.

9. A cup is a hollow which cannot decide whether to open or close, to reveal itself or to hide.

10. The cup gambles, balancing between two waters or two continents at the same time. It is pretty, but a liar.

11. A glass is a fearsome hollow; frightened to lose its contents.

12. A glass stretches upward, apprehensive.

13. With its insolent aspect, the glass assumes a false arrogance.

14. If the glass lets itself be carried away by fear or self-importance, it closes, becomes a bottle; a scar rises like a knot. A navel.

15. When a glass totters, who knows the reason why my life oscillates, filled with astonishment.

16. In the narrow neck of the bottle — like a shut purse, a sealed sex — are neither words nor fellow-feeling in common. There is a measure to guard, a pip or seed to keep hidden. The glass seals itself not only for protection. It doesn't want to share, unless they pay the price.

17. When a plate breaks something essential collapses. Love or the family. Whatever promise or pact. Whatever embrace. Even the kiss withers. It knows the worst.

18. To be startled or frightened: to have eyes as wide as plates.

19. On the surface of a plate I can see the sky of my house or of the world. The Tao begins in a plate or in the hand. Then comes the balcony.

20. On the surface of a plate I can find, in white shadow, your face.

21. There is a white shadow on the plate, a pale shadow in the polished depth. A phantom that watches me every day from the glaze.

22. In the measured hollow of a plate are your hollows, the centimetres of your bite, the hidden hour of digestion.

23. Close to the plate, the knife praises the toothed gum.

24. Close to the plate, the fork stays silent, devious and alert, like the devil's gaze.

25. In its innocuous way, the spoon licks the soup with its little gloomy complicit face.

26. In its round expanse, the plate observes you; draws you into it.

27. The plate has the blindness of eyes glazed white. You were the needle of its gaze aimed at the quarry.

28. A plate is the cloud of smoke from a cannon or the glow a corpse emits. Consider this well.

29. In the centre of the plate you place, naively and gently, the meat of a bull, a pig or a lamb. Do you believe it? Do you imagine that the fierce laws of saliva that poisons or teeth that rend and tear do not apply to you?

30. In the centre of the plate you place the speed of a lettuce. The air blows on the greenness.

31. In the dining room you listen to the hammer, the shudder, the dread, the drum of the plates.

32. In the centre of the plate see how the zebras unravel into black white fibres. On each plate there is an African motif. The lion is on the prowl.

33. The plate supports the bull, the lamb and the large green leaf, revealed between shriek and canine tooth.

34. The plate appears a surface, but it is the snare of a withdrawn purse. A claw like a bloody gauntlet. A belly.

35. From childhood I saw the white shadow of the plate and yearned to plunge into its muddy lake of blood.

36. The plate is a carnivorous plant.

37. By that plant you measure your hunger and thirst; the weight and length of your step; the kilos of pressure in your bite.

38. To sit down to eat with someone, to be at table, to make a gentle or brutal clatter of plates: to represent the digestion inside in the theatre outside.

39. The sounds from my belly and yours at this moment were our words of love two hours ago in front of our plates.

40. On the surface of the table glistens the mute depth of my plate, its blue sound pierces my mouth.

41. I look at your eyes; I look at you hungrily; I look at you with my mouth. I want to contain you; let me embrace you with my belly.

42. When we say 'I love you' or 'I want you' we do not mean the smile or the hair, much less the shoulder; it would be better to speak as we speak in the silence of the bed or the bath. Feelings make me a liar.

43. In the dominion of the plate I can say: I need to smell your foot, taste your sour unfolding armpit, inhale the grave-pits of your hot neck, touch the ring of your body, eat you, eat from your hollows. Gnaw your bone, your inside. Let me.

44. When we no longer love, then we do not eat together nor eat each other. The theatre of outside displaces the interior theatre. We are not a plate that races at the furious pace of its pleasure but rather a glass tightening itself without accent or rhyme.

45. On a plate you do not only put your food; you place the ounces and inches of your body. Your flesh and your bones. Most of all, your hollows.

46. An equation: desire = hunger, or the opposite; but perhaps this would be far better: love = plate = mouth = belly.

47. The plate is an open mouth. Feed it.

48. Under my nose, in front of my eyes, I watched two snails become two mouths on my plate. It was the most passionate kiss in the history of cinema.

49. I think of you and divide you with the cutlery of my tongue. No need for spoon or fork or knife.

50. The plate is your mouth when you come close to me. I listen to the beads of your little teeth.

51. The plate teaches me your most delicious hollow. That is why I dabble my finger in your dinner.

52. When I kiss your mouth, I kiss your deepest hollow. And I know where it starts and where it ends.

53. It is not your eyes, not your nose, not your ears which have this depth, this emptiness which encloses me and fills me. Your words, your tongue, are my witness.

54. Give me food from your plate, surrender your internal world, give me your hunger.

55. Now comes my mouth to your plate to eat from your hand.

56. I put half a tomato on the plate's surface: I see in you the insolent crest of a white cock inspecting his domain. Complacently counting the cows and chickens.

57. I place a sprig of dill on my plate; I watch your hand grow over my hand.

58. – I go to the market. I snatch olives from the counter; tear off three branches; let my eyes move along the immobile swiftness of a salmon, frozen into the oceanic vessel of sweet ice in the Fish and Seafood department. The spur of a shark, the claws of a crab. I order three pieces.

I return, laden, to my house. A full bag.

On a slow fire, for not more than twenty minutes, I cook my catch. Prepare it for you. Butter. Two sprigs of dill. You will like it.

Come, nearer, hear this music of blood and fire, eat with me. Come to my house, sit down to eat at my table. Let me enter into you, before I enter you.

59. Your plate is a delicious grave. Bury me.

Fin

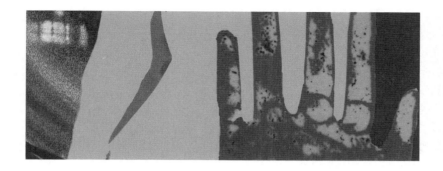

An extract from Bernard O'Donoghue's translation of *Sir Gawain and the Green Knight*

Transgresssion in *Sir Gawain*

It might seem that the idea of sexual transgression lies at the heart of all Arthurian romance, as it often does in the huge scope of Greek tragedy. After all, the ideal brotherhood of the Round Table is destroyed finally by the revelation that Queen Guinevere is involved in a thirty-year-long *amour* with Lancelot, the greatest knight in the fellowship of her husband King Arthur. Similarly, the affair of Tristan with Iseult, the wife of his lord and uncle King Mark, is the great love-tragedy of the Middle Ages and maybe of the whole western literary tradition.

Yet those grandly adulterous relationships, with their epic political dimensions, do not carry the frisson of personal transgression, in the way that it is found in an unlikely Arthurian setting. With Lancelot and Tristan, the whole story turns on the grand tragedy. But the late medieval Northern English poem *Sir Gawain and the Green Knight* is made up of a mosaic of stories paralleled elsewhere in the unreal world of romance: a green man who can speak when his head has been cut off, beautiful and loathly ladies, and magic castles. But at the heart of this web of improbabilities comes an extraordinary scene of sexual temptation, one that we have not been prepared for in the least. While Gawain is being entertained with lavish hospitality by a generous lord, a strange 'exchange of winnings' is proposed: for each of three winter days the lord will go out hunting while Gawain stays behind in the warmth and luxury of the castle. At the end of each day they will exchange what they have gained in the course of the day. Gawain, it seems, is being teased in this 'gomen', this light-hearted game: clearly the lord will have some hunted beast to offer Gawain. But what can Gawain possibly gain in the lord's castle to give in exchange? What can he gain that does not belong to the lord already?

We soon discover that it is something that can not easily be given to the lord of the castle in exchange. The lord's beautiful wife offers herself to Gawain. Something similar happens in other romances. But nowhere else do we find anything like the suggestiveness of the lady's approach to Gawain's bed, in lines 1178–1306 (printed below). It is hard to think of another text in which a conventional scene gets so far beyond the conventional. The scene has all the evocation of a modern male fantasy, but without the least sense of seediness.

Gawain is lying in bed, warm and naked, when he hears a 'little din' at his bedroom door. He lifts the corner of his bed-hangings and peeps out: 'it was the lady!' He ducks back down and pretends to be asleep. She steals inside the curtains and sits down 'softly on the bedside', waiting for him to wake up. After a while Gawain says to himself it would be more 'seemly' to admit to being awake. He opens his eyes, looks towards her and pretends to be surprised. She says he is an unwary sleeper, since it is so easy to creep up on him, and that she will 'bind' him in his bed. Gawain suggests that he could sustain this conversation more decorously if she would let him get dressed. But she says this is not necessary: her husband and his men are out hunting, all the household servants are asleep, including her ladies, and she has fastened the door with a strong lock. Since she has here the man that all ladies yearn for, she will take the opportunity. And she concludes, in a phrase that commentators (like Yeats's 'Scholars': 'old learned, respectable bald heads' that we are) have anxiously glossed away as 'conventional', 'you are welcome to my body'.

This last phrase captures exactly how the scene operates so disturbingly and suggestively, on the border of the conventional and the real. Romance is the classic escapist form; but romance-readers do not usually project themselves into the dreamworld they are reading about. What the Gawain-poet does here is much more like the procedure of the satirist, in taking to its logical conclusion what the reader's interest guiltily implies, and it leaves the reader as uncomfortable as Gawain. Gawain feels shame, and we share that sense of guilt at illicit attractiveness. And at the end, of course, it almost causes *him* to lose his head, literally.

From *Sir Gawain and the Green Knight*, lines 1178–1306

While the lord was busy by the borders of the wood
the bold Gawain kept to his soft bed.
He lay there till daylight shone on the walls,
beneath his bright bedspread, screened all around.
As he dozed there in peace, he warily heard
a little noise at the door as it stealthily opened.
He raised his head up out of the clothes
and slightly lifted the edge of the curtain,
peeping out cautiously to see what it was.
It was the lady, most lovely to look at,
who shut the door after her, in secret and privately,

and stole towards the bed. The hero, embarrassed,
lay hurriedly back down, pretending to sleep.
She stepped forward silently and stole to his bedside,
lifted the curtain and crept inside,
sitting down softly on the edge of the bed.
And there she stayed, to see if he'd wake up.
The hero lay low some considerable time,
pondering inwardly what all this might mean
or amount to. It seemed pretty strange,
but still he said to himself, 'It would be more fitting
to ask her openly what she is after.'
So he awoke, and stretched and, turning towards her,
opened his eyes, pretending to be surprised.
Then, as if to be safer by prayer, he blessed himself
                        with his hand.
            With her pretty chin, and cheeks
            of mingled red and white,
            she spoke most sweetly
            with her small, laughing lips.

'Good morning, Sir Gawain,' said the lovely lady,
'you're a careless sleeper, to let someone creep
up on you like this. You're caught. Unless there's a truce,
I'll besiege you in bed, you can be sure.'
Laughing away she made jokes like that.
'Good morning, fair lady,' said Gawain, all good humour.
'I am at your service, and delighted to be so;
I surrender at once and sue for mercy:
the best policy since I have no option.'
And so he joked in return, with cheerful laughter.
'But if, lovely lady, you'd grant me this –
to release your prisoner, and ask him to stand,
I'd get out of this bed and dress myself better;
I would talk to you then in the greatest comfort.'
'No indeed, handsome sir,' the fair lady said,
'you are not getting up. I've a better plan for you.

I'll besiege you on the other flank too
and then negotiate with my knight that I've caught;
because I know well that you are Sir Gawain
that the whole world worships wherever you go.
Your honour and accomplishment are highly praised
by lords and by ladies and by everyone living.
And here you are now, and just us two.
My husband and his men are gone far afield;
everyone else is in bed; my ladies are too.
The door is shut, securely locked.
Since I have in my house everyone's favourite,
I will spend my time well, as long as it lasts,
                    in talk.
              You are welcome to my body
              to exercise your power.
              I am obliged, and willing,
              to bend to your greater strength.'

'Well,' said Gawain, 'this is a privilege,
but I am far from what you describe.
I am unworthy to rise to such honour
as you suggest here; I know myself well.
If such was your wish, by God I'd be pleased
if I might be of service in word or in deed
to serve your good will it would be pure joy.'
'Now truly, Sir Gawain,' said the beautiful lady,
'if I should undervalue the prowess and standing
that please everyone else, it would be no credit.
There are plenty of women who would much rather have
you, noble sir, as I have you here,
interchanging fine words with you,
to bring them comfort and soothe their cares,
than most of the treasure or goods that they have.
But I praise the lord that rules the high heavens
that I've here in my hands what everyone wants
                    by the sheerest good fortune.'

She, of such beauty,
was so flattering to him,
and the knight with proper speech
replied to all she said.

'Madame,' said Gawain, 'may Our Lady reward you,
for your kindness to me is generous indeed.
But people often form judgments on rumour,
and I do not deserve the acclaim that they give.
It is to your credit that you think only goodness.'
'By Mary,' the lady said, 'I don't believe that;
for if I were as worthy as any woman living,
and all the wealth of the world were at my disposal,
and I bargained for ever to find a good partner,
from your behaviour that I have seen here –
your good looks and grace and kindly demeanour
(which I'd heard of before and now find to be true) –
no man on earth would be chosen before you.'
'Noble lady,' he said, 'you're certainly matched better.
But still I am honoured by your good opinion
and, as your humble servant, I hold you my ruler
and declare myself your knight. May Christ reward you!'
So they talked on till past the mid-morning,
with the lady acting as if she loved him.
The knight held his ground and behaved very well,
considering her beauty and what she'd in mind.
There was less love in him because of the hardship
            he'd shortly to face,
        the blow that will strike him,
        as it must come about.
        So when she spoke of leaving,
        he readily agreed.

Then she bade him good day and glanced at him, laughing.
But as she stood up, her fierce words appalled him.
'May whoever rewards talking repay you for this;

but that you are Gawain can not be believed.'
'Why?' said the knight in eager enquiry,
afraid he'd come short in some detail of manners.
The lady blessed him and said, 'For this reason:
someone who is reputed as accomplished as Gawain,
with manners developed so perfectly in him,
could hardly have sat so long with a lady
without begging a kiss in the name of courtesy,
by some hint or other at the end of conversing.'
Then Gawain said, 'Please, let us do what you wish:
I will kiss at your command, as a knight's duty is,
and do more rather than offend you, so don't ask again.'
She came near and took him within her arms,
bending down sweetly, and kissed her hero.

Bernard O'Donoghue's translation of *Sir Gawain and the Green Knight* will be published in Penguin Classics, August 2006.

W.D. Jackson, Two extracts from a work-in-progress: *Boccaccio in Florence: Three Stories and a Dream*, *translated and adapted from The Decameron*

'So from Chaucer I was led to think on Boccacce, . . . the Genius of our Countrymen being rather to improve an Invention, than to invent themselves; . . . yet it appears that the Tales of Boccacce were not generally of his own making, but taken from Authors of former Ages, and by him only modell'd . . .' Dryden, Preface to *Fables Ancient and Modern* (1699).

Although he seems to have suffered some sort of conversion around the age of fifty and, in later life, came increasingly under the influence of the rather strait-laced Petrarch, who encouraged him in the writing of humanistic treatises in Latin, Boccaccio's earlier work in the vernacular, above all *The Decameron* (1349–50), took a very different view of social or Christian mores and those who transgressed them from that of either Petrarch himself (whose reputation as a moralist as well as a poet was already flourishing) or Dante, their common master. This liberality or licentiousness, depending on how you look at it, was not confined to sexual relations, as the first of the two stories below illustrates, but these are predominant (as everyone knows) in Boccaccio's work. Dante, of course, was famous for idealizing his love of Beatrice (as Petrarch later idealized Laura) and for plunging Paolo and Francesca into the Second Circle of Hell for so slight a crime as adultery – not to mention Brunetto Latini and the sodomites further down. In *The Decameron*, on the other hand, while there is certainly an official morality, which is all right in its way, anyone with any sense doesn't pay it too much attention. And so almost anything goes: adultery is implicitly recommended to anyone bored with their spouse, clerics would be fools if they didn't make the most of any gift which the good Lord places in their path (I,iv), and all kinds of sexual excess, oddity and perversion (as it used to be called) are not so much condoned as taken for granted and enjoyed. In fact, the only serious sexual transgressions, if one can call them that, in Boccaccio's view seem to be possessiveness or jealousy (usually that of elderly husbands with young wives) and abstemiousness of one sort or another (usually, again, of elderly husbands or, above all, as preached and sometimes even practised by the Church). Typically, an unsatisfactory husband will be outsmarted by a better man and the wife and her lover will discreetly continue to enjoy their illicit love. Nor is there the slightest hint of irony when Boccaccio ends such stories, as he often does, with some phrase like 'May God grant that we enjoy ours likewise' (III, vi).

Apart from personal inclination, one possible reason for such changes in moral attitude between Dante (1265–1321) and Boccaccio (1313–1375) may well have been the appearance of the plague and in particular the Black Death, which reached Italy from Asia in 1347. Of the plague at this time and later, it has been said that only the most obstinately devout could have seen its unprecedented horror, its seemingly arbitrary appearances and disappearances, as part of some Dantesque or medieval divine plan. And it is obviously significant in this respect that Boccaccio starts *The Decameron* with a description of the Black Death or 'magna mortalitas', as it came to be known, which he claims to have witnessed in Florence. While Boccaccio does not go so far as directly to question the social or religious fabric of medieval society, he sometimes comes remarkably close to doing so and an unmistakable atmosphere of *carpe diem* permeates the whole framework as well as the individual stories of *The Decameron*, in which ten young people retire from the plague-infested city of Florence to the countryside, where each of them tells one tale per day in idyllic surroundings which are beautifully – almost surrealistically – evoked. The first of the following translations/adaptations – of II,v (the second is of III,i) – incorporates passages from Boccaccio's introductory description and imagines how the whole collection might have started, but presumably didn't. Boccaccio's prose is transposed into the 'Venus and Adonis' stanza and Chaucerian couplets respectively because both Shakespeare and Chaucer borrowed – directly or indirectly – not only stories but aspects of their world-view from their great precursor. So much so that a number of lines from both of them have transgressed into these versions. If at the end of his life Boccaccio returned to the Dantesque vision of things (in his *Life of Dante* and commentary on the first seventeen cantos of the *Divina Commedia*), so did Chaucer in his so-called Retractation at the end of *The Canterbury Tales*. In more recent times one need go no further than Tolstoy to find an author turning against his own earlier writings. And there are, of course, many parallel instances not only in the history of literature but of societies in general – as anyone who was young in 1968 and has survived into the age of Aids will be aware. Whether humanity will ever make much actual progress between transgressing and regressing in such matters remains to be seen. Unfortunately, the twenty-first century's plague seems unlikely to encourage much liberation in the popular mind.

I
The Dream

'Al quale ella, quasi ridendo disse: "Buon uomo, el mi par
che tu sogni."'
          Decameron II,v

May, 1348. The sun was sinking
Behind the campanile. Boccaccio knelt
Inside the still unfinished duomo, thinking
Of what he'd seen, and wondering how he felt
About the Immortal Architect . . . Could He
Have planned this plague, this 'Great Mortality'?

Whole houses, great palazzi, emptied of
Their occupants, the dead piled up outside
With oozing tumours. Rat-packs freely roved
Deserted streets, where pigs and dogs had died
From mauling corpses or infected rags,
And looters staggered under bursting bags.

Abandoned children cried. The sick were left
To die alone, their bodies left to rot.
The stench of dead or dying people bereft
Him of all words. But some he knew were not
So easily shocked. All forms of strange excess
Flourished helped stave off horror and distress.

Men dropped down dead in the street by day and night.
Coffins and grave-plots were a rarity.
Rough gangs of paupers dug deep plague-pits right
Across old churchyards, charging a fat fee
To stow the dead in tiers with a thin layer
Of soil between. And more for a priest or a prayer.

But most were thrown in like dead goats or sheep . . .
Which stopped him trying to pray. Instead, he sat
And closed his aching eyes, and fell asleep,
And dreamt he'd travelled home to Naples — at
The market, where he'd come to buy a horse.
But all the horses were half-dead, or worse.

And all their grooms and riders were half-dead
And putrefying slowly. Stinking meat,
Alive with maggots, and the grinning head
Of a huge boar, were all there was to eat.
One stall had bursting figs, egg-plants, milk, honey,
But no one left alive to take his money.

And so he waved his bulging bag of gold
To bring them back to life: five hundred florins.
A pretty girl strolled past. From how she strolled
He knew she'd like to go with him to Florence.
She smiled and said she was his bastard sister.
I'm illegitimate too, he cried, and kissed her.

Safe in her rooms, she wore a veil-like dress
With living leaves and slowly opening flowers
Which he could see straight through. In less
Than no time he'd been there for hours and hours.
Her black eyes flashed. Fresh fruit and roasted meat
And wine appeared. OK, she laughed, let's eat.

And so they ate, drank, laughed, till very late.
As children we'd have shared a double bed,
She giggled coyly. Let's not curse our fate
But make up for it now. He gawped. She said,
Although we had one dad, a different womb
Had us . . . Or would you like a separate room?

My sweet, she whispered, now I've got you here
Locked in my soft white arms, within their pale,
I'll be a park and you can be my deer,
Feed where you want to feed, up hill down dale,
Graze on my lips, or if their slopes are dry
Look lower, where my rough moist-pastures lie.

At this he smiled and, since the night was hot,
They took each other's clothes off, kissed and groped,
And tried it standing up before they got
Into her bed. But, as she must have hoped,
He wanted to relieve himself before
Proceeding. Over there, she said. That door.

And off he dashed. Outside a loosened plank
Shot up and he shot down into the filth
Of many years. The next house was a bank,
In which his father sat, while his own wealth
Was counted by the old man's bastard daughter.
He closed his eyes. A stream of lukewarm water

Splashed off his chest. Shrieking with laughter, high
On the one remaining plank spanning the alley,
She squatted till she'd finished. That pig-sty
's the perfect place for you, she whooped. You wally!
He scraped away both fresh and ancient dirt.
No broken bones. But now his pride was hurt.

And, leaping the six-foot wall which separated
Sump from road, he found his sister's door –
Where he yelled and banged in vain. Infuriated,
And feeling very nude, he banged and swore
At the blank windows. Till her sleepy bully
Opened one, dropped his clothes out, and said dully

Wake me again, friend, and I'll knock you cold.
The thick black beard and scars of this tough guy
Convinced his doxy's brother that the gold
Was gone for good. He raged. But, rather than die
On his sister's door-step, donned his shoes and shirt
And stumped off down the road, stinking of dirt.

But which, and where, was his inn? Beside the sea?
This was no town for wandering round at night.
Two hulks approached. Cut-throats perhaps. So he,
Exposed and helpless, side-stepped out of sight
Into a hut. But in they stepped as well.
By Christ, they huffed and phewed, what's that foul smell?

Holding his nose, one raised their dingy lamp,
Which lit up B., who, trapped and trembling, told
His tale of woe, inspiring them to thump
His dirt-caked back. You'd have lost more than gold,
They sniggered, if you'd dozed off in that bed.
Now come and help us crack a tomb instead.

The archbishop's dead, and buried in full regalia.
His ruby ring alone is worth five hundred
Florentine florins. B. noted, inter alia,
This ring could save his face, and also wondered
How much the bishop's vestments might be worth,
And all the other stuff he'd left on earth.

The only problem is, they groaned, you smell
Worse than a cess-pit, or like putrid flesh.
But halfway to the duomo there's a well
We'll let you down in. Then, if you smell fresh
Enough for church, we'll show you how to rob
Its rich to feed the poor. A damned good job!

So at the well they made him mount the bucket,
And wound him down until he hit the water.
Just then — a piece of filthy rotten luck — it
Chanced that the watch, checking that run-down quarter,
Felt like a drink. The fly-by-nights did a flit,
Leaving their new friend stuck once more in the shit.

As he knew, and didn't know. Once down he drank
His fill before performing his ablutions.
Up went the bucket. But the water stank.
The watch suspected poison or pollution:
Perhaps a murdered corpse. Then B.'s wet head
Popped over the rim of the well. They howled and fled.

B. scanned their lethal weapons. Could his inn
Be somehow in the duomo? His two friends
Smiled yes it could — began, then, to break in
To where the bishop lay. To make amends
For running off, they grinned, they'd let poor B.
Enter the grave and say what he could see.

The vault had one immensely heavy lid
Of marble. Flights of stone-cold marble stairs
Faded to where a foetid darkness hid
The archbishop and the bones of his forebears.
B. reeled, and retched in horror. But they said,
You go in there alive, or go in dead.

Shaking with fear, B. squeezed into the hole
They'd levered open. First he stole the ring
And hid it in his pocket. Then he stole
The bishop's crozier, mitre, everything
Worth snitching he could hand them from the body.
Naked, Monsignor looked a proper noddy.

But where's the ring? the furious bully-boys
Hissed down. It must be somewhere. Look again!
B. looked, until an unexpected noise
Of footsteps made the burglars change their plan.
Humping their swag, they scarpered quickly. But
First they dislodged their jemmies. The lid slammed shut.

B. couldn't budge it. Overcome with fear,
He fainted by the faintly glowing stiff.
Recovered, he was sure he'd starve in there
Or go stark staring mad. And even if
They disinterred him, he'd still come to grief.
The grave was robbed, and he'd be hanged as a thief.

Or could it be he was already dead?
The air was blacker than the blackest ink,
Drowning all words, flooding B.'s silent head.
He cried out loud. His cry and the stifling stink
Of dusty death must mean he hadn't died –
As must the night-watch, now arrived outside . . .

And then, within his dream, in some strange way
B. realized he was dreaming – only dreaming.
Which means that I don't really have to stay
In here, he thought. In fact, I'll try re-dreaming
Those voices into – what? Another gang?
I'm not dead yet. Death's sickle can go hang.

And so the gang heaved up the heavy lid,
But no big bravo wanted to go in.
A priest among them sneered and sleekly slid
His legs through, jumping out of his snake's skin
When B. grabbed hold of them, and started to haul
Him down into the grave – legs, arse and all.

The priest began to kick and then to yell.
B. held on tight. The gangsters howled and fled.
Like a black flapping crow released from hell,
The priest fled too. Thus, very far from dead,
With the ring now on his finger, self-endowed
With life and luck, Boccaccio laughed out loud

And woke. Before him in the thickening dark
A group of girls were laughing with three men
About another girl called Alibech.
Boccaccio counted altogether ten,
As Filostrato begged Fiammetta's pardon
For telling one about a convent garden . . .

Boccaccio listened – couldn't help but smile . . .
Nastagio degli Onesti's heartless way
With women next beguiled them for a while.
Outside the plague still raged. Ten people. Say
Each told ten stories. Three plus one makes four,
To start with. Which makes ninety-six tales more . . .

II
The Convent Garden

Not far from Florence lies a convent, whose
Nuns are devout, whose panoramic views
Are justly famous – but which we won't name,
For fear of spoiling so much well-earned fame . . .
Its ancient gardener, Nuto, who had come
From elsewhere, now felt ripe for going home
To doze beneath his neighbours' apple-trees

In gardens where no jumpy nuns could tease
Or tell him off or giggle and hide his tools.
– 'They'd blare like ewes on heat. A flock of fools!'
He'd crudely croak, once home, to anyone
Who'd listen: 'Never cross a rutting nun.'
Then Nuto died. His neighbour was a young
Mild-mannered man whose older wife's sharp tongue
Was often heard excoriating him.
Masetto was his name – tall, strong, and slim
About the hips and buttocks. When they buried
Old Nuto, young Masetto had been married
For just two years. Two years which seemed two lives.
He stared at all the wrinkled, withered wives
Whose men were mouldering corpses. A last few
Were staggering under the bier. 'There's nothing new,'
Masetto thought, 'in heaven or earth. What fun
It must be, though, to do it with a nun!'
But now the dead man's brothers were in tears:
'A few more years they have, just a few years.
One woman brought them in. Another woman
Will see them out. Poor Nuto's case is common.
But not for me, no thank you, not just yet!
At break of day tomorrow, off I set. –
For though it's been no more than two short years,
God knows I've wept tin buckets full of tears
Since feeding at the trough of married life.
Some praise its pleasures, but my loud-mouthed wife
Has caused me nothing but expense and trouble.
Conjugal bliss? I've pricked that bitter bubble!
And yet, God also knows, the neighbours say –
Particularly the women, by the way –
My wife is true and steadfast, the best kind
Of cheerful helpmate you could hope to find.
But he who wears the shoe knows where it pinches.
At first she praised me for my extra inches:
Too big for her I was, or so she claimed –

And humped me like a rabbit. Till, well-tamed,
I married her. But, only shortly after,
I was the butt of her and her friends' laughter.
The rows we've had! It does no good to curse her.
I'll knock her flat one day. Or vice versa.
She thought I was a big, soft, harmless brute.
High time I went! She'll like the extra loot.
When I first saw her hard face at our fair,
I thought she was a thief, if not a whore;
And though she's made me want her, if the truth
Were told about my wife, I'd say she's both.'

Next evening, at the convent's kitchen door,
Masetto stood pretending to be poor
And begged with hand-signs, as if born deaf-mute.
The convent being a house of good repute,
This subterfuge, he hoped, would get him in
By prompting thoughts of virtue, not of sin.
The steward eyed his rags and read his signs,
But not his mind, and thought, 'Before he dines,
I'll give this big strong lout those logs to chop
Which Nuto couldn't.' Masetto chopped non-stop,
Hoicking enormous bundles on his back
And storing the wood in one long tidy stack
Against the kitchen wall beneath the eaves.
'There's more that he could do before he leaves,'
The steward pressed the abbess. 'Let him stay
For now,' she sang, 'and get stuck in. In May
Hedges, weeds, lawns, need seeing to twice a week.
A deaf-mute shouldn't give the girls much cheek!
Be sure he gets a decent pair of pants.'
Masetto eavesdropped, rubbing his red hands,
And laughed: 'Your flowers and bushes shall be more
Thoroughly seen to now than ever before!'
First, though, he sought to please his two new bosses,
Clipped, weeded, mowed, scrubbed mosses from the crosses

Stationed upon the convent's Calvary.
At length the ageing steward left him free
To organize his work at his own pace.
One day, in a secluded shady place,
Masetto saw two very young nuns peeping
Around a bush, assuming he was sleeping.
The day before they'd laughed till they were puce
Using the sort of words nice nuns don't use –
Which he, of course, pretended not to hear.
The bolder one said, 'I've had an idea
I'd tell you if I thought you'd keep it quiet –
To add some spice to our dull daily diet
Of fasting, Latin prayers and meditation.
The hottest spice, they say, is copulation.
This big strong lad's deaf, mute and also dim:
So why not try how hot it is with him?'
The other gasped: 'But what about our vows?
And what if we got pregnant?' – 'Use your nous,'
The younger scoffed: 'As long as no one knows,
What difference does it make?' After three goes
With M. behind the tool-shed, she confirmed
The truth of all she'd heard. The coy one squirmed
And dithered, but then – not to be outdone –
Next afternoon she also had her fun;
And from then on they missed no chance to enjoy
The age-old pleasures of their big new toy.
Until one day an older sister, viewing
The Tuscan landscape, spotted all three screwing
Like mad down at the bottom of the garden:
Amazed by dumb Masetto's hefty hard-on,
Her eyes alone asked two more sisters – brought
To witness this *ménage à trois* – what ought
They now to do: inform the abbess – or . . . ?
'Perhaps he'd welcome one or two nuns more,'
The shyest simpered, as they watched. And that
Knocked all their scruples into a cocked hat.

They waited till the three had finished dogging —
Giggling like blushing virgins, even snogging
A bit — and then went down to claim their share
In dim dumb strong Masetto: fair was fair.
The convent housed eight nuns in all, and so
Soon the remaining three were in the know.
They all took turns at riding hell-for-leather,
While staunch Masetto braced himself to weather
This storm of nuns, unholy and unholier.
Asleep one morning by the great magnolia,
Whose lemon-scented blossom filled the shade
With sweet, narcotic perfume — newly laid,
Masetto was observed by the abbess
In an embarrassing state of some undress,
And, though she was a serious-minded nun,
When he began to stiffen in the sun,
Dreaming no doubt of what he'd just been having,
Her gawp became a gaze, till the same craving
To which her younger charges had succumbed
Grabbed her as well. Her Bible was well-thumbed —
But no help now. Plucking him like a flower,
She woke and led him to her cell, or bower,
In whose snug privacy she dared to savour
The vice she'd always viewed with most disfavour,
For several days. The nuns soon comprehended
Why work on their own gardens was suspended
And, bitterly complaining to their Mother
Superior, failed to comfort one another.
But she and he ploughed on. And even if
Masetto's tool was less than keen or stiff,
She still knew how to get the greens she wanted.
Her gardener dug, drilled, seeded, puffed and panted,
Though in the flabby end, afraid lest he
Should do himself some serious injury,
He blurted out, 'Please stop now, ma'am. I've heard
One cock will do for ten hens. But, no bird,

You need at least ten men! And here am I
Also required to serve and satisfy
Another eight. It's heaven on earth. But, please,
To carry on, I need to stand at ease
A little.' – 'Ha!' she piped. 'Why aren't you dumb?'
'I was, ma'am. But, you see, the more I've come
With you and all the other nuns, the less
I've felt stone-deaf and tongue-tied.' The abbess,
Recalling how the sisters had been miffed
To lose their gardener, feeling somewhat biffed
By all these revelations, sat down quickly
But, in a moment, started smiling slickly –
Painfully aware that what was happening here
Could terminate her promising career.
Masetto smiled as well: the steward had died
Not long before – perhaps they could decide
On some arrangement which would suit them all?
If no one knew beyond the garden wall,
What difference would it make? And so their neighbours
Were told Masetto's prayers and saintly labours
Of horticultural love, plus the nuns' fasting
And holy tears, had moved the Everlasting
To unlock his tongue and open his blocked ears.
Masetto worked as steward for many years,
Helped by the nuns, and helped them in return
To lead a pleasant life and not to burn.
He also sometimes visited his wife,
Who was not unimpressed by his new life
Of prosperous piety. The girls and boys
He fathered were the secret pride and joy
Of all the convent, cared for by the nuns'
Families. Masetto raced his riotous sons
Around the garden, gave his daughters cherries –
Showed them where they could gather nuts, plums, berries,
And played at hide-and-seek . . . Till, finally,
The good abbess retired, and so did he,

Discreetly bribed with a fat monthly pension.
His wife now welcomed his well-off attention –
A sweet reversal of their former roles
(Though still involving neither of their souls) –
For she was hot, who used to be so cold,
'Though what,' he wondered, 'when she gets too old?'

Helen Constantine
Banned Poems

The newly-planted trees along the Cowley Road in Oxford are reluctant to open their buds this cold spring. Shoppers are cheered instead by the multi-coloured tapestries of graffiti decorating walls and hoardings on the shops and medical centre. Walk a little way along past the octopuses and seaweed on the public lavatories and you will notice that someone has erased a poem from one wall, leaving just the images that accompanied it. We print the story in pictures, then the offending poem, below.

The original mural

The censored wall

Artists' comment and the Three Wise Monkeys

The offending poem:

The Myth of Third World Debt

I hear tell
that the 'West' claims
'Third World' countries
owe them a debt.

The white people them
they come to our countries
they unleash
upon we
the holocaust of slavery
the evil, parasitic, violent process
them call colonization.

What this means is
them rape Mother Africa
took her children to use as donkey
went right inside Mother Africa belly
and steal her resources
send them back home
to the 'West'.

We the Africans,
funded the industrial revolution
with our blood, sweat, and tears and
Life.

So I don't really understand
what the 'West' means
when them talk 'bout 'Third World debt'
I believe them have no shame
I know they full of untruth
they lie to themselves constantly
cause truth will kill them fe true.

I ask you to reconsider
who owes whom?

The West owes Africa
a debt so great
them can never
fully repay.

Though we may not say it,
don't think we do not see it
We are silent
because white men talk too much
all in aid
of hiding the truth.

Third world debt
is a fiction of
white mans imagination.

Nyarai Humba

These photographs can be found at:
www.indymedia.org.uk/en/regions/oxford/2005/12/
330357.html

There is no greater testimony to the power of the word than a banned poem or song. A poem has the capacity to inspire terror in the most tyrannical of despots and fear in the heart of the most formidable of undemocratic and sometimes even democratic governments. It may frequently land its writer in gaol, and expose him or her to torture, or worse. The poems of Akhmatova were banned in Russia between 1925–40 and 1946–56; the poet Osip Mandelstam died in the Camps in 1938; the songs of the Greek writer and composer, Mikis Theodorakis, were banned under the Colonels (1967–72), and he was imprisoned and maltreated; Miroslav Holub's 'The Prague of Jan Palach' was not allowed to be published in Czech, but was published by the *TLS* in English translation in 1969. We might also mention the work of Marin Sorescu, Irina Ratushinskaya and, more recently, poems by Turkish, Iraqi, Burmese poets that have been suppressed by the authorities. A Turkish schoolboy was arrested and detained for a short time last year for reciting a poem by a dissident poet at a school concert; and even in so-called liberal countries you may find yourself in trouble with the law if you express your opinions too freely. It emerged recently that MI5 'kept watch on' the folk singer Ewan MacColl (and his wife, Joan Littlewood) because he was suspected of expressing communist sympathies in his songs.

If all of these poets may be said to have transgressed in the legal sense, they form part of a noble tradition – noble because it so often symbolizes the triumph of the spirit over brute force – of dissident poets who dare to speak the truth in a society which is finding it more and more difficult to do so.

Poems may be banned for a variety of reasons: political, religious, moral.

Six poems in Baudelaire's *Fleurs du Mal* were censored because of their subject matter – sex – and the publication of the whole collection resulted in a prosecution for obscenity and blasphemy. Two of the censored poems are translated here.

Lethe

Your soul is deaf to mine and cruel but lie
Tigerish, indolent monster I adore,
Here on my heart, I wish to steep and steady
My hands in the heavy thicket of your hair

Or in your skirts, that smell of you, entomb
My head full of the dolorous hurts you gave
And breathe in what's still left of love, its grave
And after-smell, its over-opened bloom.

I want to sleep, more than I want to live,
In a sleep as soft on me as death would be
And lay my kisses like one glad to give
The length of you who are smooth and coppery.

To swallow up my sobbing when it stops
There's nowhere better than your bed's deep pit;
At the waters of your mouth I can forget;
You slip me Lethe through your parting lips.

I will obey my fate, henceforth my bliss,
The way the elect, the predestined, do,
As docile martyr, condemned innocent, who
Self-stokes the hot pyre hotter with holiness;

And drown my bitterness by sucking good
Hemlock and nepenthes at the tart
Points of your tight breasts that never did
Under their charms contain a captive heart.

The Jewels

She I love much was nude except that she,
Knowing my likings, had kept her jewellery on,
Which sonorous gear gave her the mastery
Slaves have on good days over their sultan.

When it flings out its quick and mocking noise
This dancing world brilliant with metal and stone
Ecstasies me, I love to madness those
Things in which light and sound combine and join.

So she lay out on high allowing me
To love her couched up there smiling at ease
Down at my love as deep and gentle as the sea
That towards her, up the cliff-face of her, rose.

Eyes fixed on me, beast in captivity,
In a dreaming absent-mindedness she tried out poses
Whose candour mixing with lubricity
Gave a new edge to her metamorphoses;

And her arms, her legs, her bum, her thighs,
Smooth as oil, swanlike, serpentine,
Displayed to my serene clear-seeing eyes,
And her belly and breasts, grape-clusters of my vine,

Came on more sweetly than the Bad Angel
And troubled the repose my soul had made
And moved her from her crystal pedestal
Where she had sat, calmly in solitude.

In a new design, her buttocks salient,
I seemed to see Antiope's thighs below
The bust of a smooth boy, magnificent
Her fauve and painted duskiness on show

And the lamp having resigned itself to die
Firelight was all the lighting that room had
And sudden flames, exhaling with a sigh,
Coloured her amber skin blood-red.

These poems were deemed to offend against public decency, just as James Kirkup's poem 'The love that dares to speak its name,' describing a centurion's homosexual fantasies about the crucified Christ, does still, apparently, in our own time. This poem, which is itself a reference to the poem 'Two Loves' by Lord Alfred Douglas, was first published in *Gay News* in 1976. A private prosecution was brought against the editor and publisher by Mary Whitehouse. They were found guilty of blasphemous libel. In 2002 eleven readers spoke one verse each on the steps of St. Martin in the Field in London, but no one was prosecuted as a result. The poem, in any case, may be easily located on various websites including www.alsopreview.com/jklove.html and a copy is freely available from Free Speech Movement, 84B Whitechapel High Street London E1 7QX. Still, we are advised that it would be risky to print the poem in this magazine, blasphemy of one sort or another being at present a dangerous matter. Homosexuality, of course, even without the religious association, is still a contentious issue in many countries around the world: Ang Lee's recent film success, *Brokeback Mountain*, on this subject, is currently banned in his own country, China, and has been the target of much criticism in others. But much more common in our own troubled times are poems that are banned because of their criticism of governments and of the human rights abuses that still take place in many prisons around the world.

The well-known poem by Boris Vian, 'Le Déserteur' was
banned in France during the war in Indo-China and again
during the war in Algeria because it was thought to be
encouraging soldiers to desert. A newspaper reports this week
that the 'President's men', thinking it will be a deterrent for
those called up to fight in Iraq, are still searching out and
arresting those who did desert during the Vietnam War forty
years ago (*Guardian*, 14.03.06). Originally Vian wrote: 'Que je
serai en arme / Et que je sais tirer', (I shall be armed/ And I
know how to pull a trigger) but he was persuaded to change
these final lines of his poem to fit its essential pacifism, and it
is the changed version which was sung all over the world by
singers such as Mouloudji and Peter, of Peter, Paul and Mary.
It has been translated into thirty-nine languages and is as
relevant today as it was when Vian wrote it.

Dear Mister President
I'm writing this letter
And maybe you'll read it
If you've nothing better
To do. Just today
I've had orders to go
Fight your war overseas
I've to leave straight away.
Dear Mister President
I sure don't want to go
We're not here below
To exterminate folks.
Sir, you know I don't wish
To cause trouble or woe
But my mind is made up
And I'm not gonna go.
My life aint been easy.
First my old man went,
Then my brothers and kids

Up and left and it sent
Momma into her grave
Dead of a broken heart
She don't give a damn now
For bombs or grenades.
While I was a prisoner
Some guy stole my woman
Stole away my soul, man,
And all I held dear.
Early in the morning
I'll lock up my doors
Shut out the dead years
Get out on the road.
I'll up and leave town
And travel on down
From the midwest to Mexico
Spreading the word
My word that says no
To your battles and wars.
I aint gonna go
And I aint gonna fight
But if *you* want to go, sir,
Take up arms tonight.
If you're after my blood
You can tell them from me,
All your President's men
That I don't have a gun.
They can shoot if they like.

Yang Lian's poem 'Banned Poem' was written after he heard
that the Chinese authorities had banned his collection of poems
Huang (*Yellow*) after the Tiananmen Square Massacre in 1989.
It was read aloud, along with poems by the Malawi poet Jack
Mapanje and the Kurdish poet Choman Hardi, at an event in
November last year in London held by Poet in the City and
Amnesty International. Yang Lian and his wife Yoyo, who
were not in China at the time of the uprising, when between
400 and 800 people were killed and many thousands injured,
immediately began a life of exile. Yang Lian has, through his
poetry and essays, continued to be critical of the Chinese
authorities, and publicized the plight of the millions of
peasants still subjected to the heavy burden of taxation in
China.

Banned Poem

to die at thirty-five is already too late
you should have been executed in the womb
like your poem

it's a shoal of eels down in the deep waters of the flesh
threading through white seaweed
among still-paler shouts you hear only darkness
coldly wiped clean by another hand
coolly turned into a misprint
placenta wrapping you ever tighter
your last words dying with you
to die today
is to be turned into a stinking news story

(*Translated by Brian Holtom*)

The poet, Nazim Hikmet, regarded as one of the most important Turkish poets in the twentieth century,was born in Salonika in 1902 and died in June 1963. He was sentenced to twenty-eight years imprisonment in 1938 on the grounds that military cadets in Turkey were being incited to revolution by reading his poetry, in particular the poem 'The Epic of Sheik Bedrettin'. Though he did not have to serve all of that sentence, Hikmet did indeed spend the next twelve years in and out of prison, and was often held in appalling conditions. At the same time his books were suppressed by the state. As Mutlu Konuk, one of his translators, says, Hikmet's prosecutors in a sense honoured him by believing that a book of poems could have such a dramatic effect. He wrote the following poem in February 1948 to Kemal Tahir from prison.

On Living

I
Life's no joke,
you must live it in earnest
    like a squirrel, for example,
expecting nothing outside your life or beyond,
    you must concentrate wholly on living.

You must take living seriously,
so much so that,
your back to the wall, your arms bound behind;
or in a laboratory
            in your white coat and big goggles
            you can die for mankind,
            even for people whose faces you've never seen,

even though nobody forces you,
even though you know the best thing, the most real,
     is to live.
You'll take living so seriously
that even at seventy, you'll plant olive trees
not just to leave to your children;
     but because, although you fear death
        you don't believe in it,
        so great is the power of life.

    II
Say we're ill enough for a major operation,
I mean that perhaps we won't ever get up
     from the white table.
If we have to feel sorry for leaving a little early,
we can still laugh at Nasreddin Hodja jokes,
and look from the window to see if it rains,
or hang around restless
     for the latest news.

Say we're fighting for something worthwhile,
     at the front, for example;
at the first assault the first day,
     we might fall face down and die.
We'll feel a strange anger,
     and not knowing
        the end of that war which could last for years
        will still drive us mad.

Say we're in prison,
our age almost fifty,
eighteen years till they open the iron door;
but we must live with the world outside,
with its people and animals, its quarrels, its wind,
     the world beyond the wall.

But wherever, however we are,
    we must live as though
    we will never die.

    III
This world will grow cold,
a star among stars,
    one of the smallest
this great world of ours
    a gilded mote on blue velvet.

This world will grow cold one day,
not even as a heap of ice,
or a lifeless cloud
it will roll like an empty walnut round and round
    in pitch darkness for ever.

For now you must feel this pain,
and endure the sadness
but so love this world
that you can say,
'I have lived'.

(Translated by Ruth Christie)

Jean Follain
Seven Poems
Translated and introduced by
Olivia McCannon

Jean Follain (1903–1971) was born in Normandy and lived through two World Wars. In the second, almost 90% of the town he grew up in, Saint-Lô, was destroyed by bombing. He wrote eight main collections of poetry and a number of prose works, including a glossary of ecclesiastical slang and a celebration of the potato. In 1927 he was called to the bar in Paris and later served as a magistrate.

In his poetry we have no sense of any rules being either made or broken, nor of any obvious artistic affiliation. We do sense a kind of innocence, an attitude of infinite receptiveness and openness, which is reflected by the absence of any persona. Interestingly, unlike many of his friends and contemporaries (such as Guillevic, Frénaud or Aragon), Follain never took the path of political *engagement*.

No structural, metrical or rhythmical expectation is set up or fulfilled in his poems. Yet this is the form he chose to express a kind of intuitive order – one which has every-thing to do with symbiotic profusion, diversity and flux and nothing to do with uniforms, fences and lines. His poems look a little like fragments, and yet we are left with a feeling of wholeness.

In all of the poems in this selection, partaking of food or drink connects with something larger: a form of ritual or exchange, a kind of secular transubstantiation, or a powerful emotion. We see how the most random experiences – the kind of unremarkable everyday events that are most easily forgotten – may be integral to the whole fabric of existence. In one cell we might find the truth of creation, in one second, infinity.

In *La Table,* Follain wrote, 'with every war, we lose another type of bread'. Characteristically, a small incident ripples out to reveal a widespread, worrying pattern of destruction and loss. The rule in his poetry is the diversity of life, constantly transgressed by the unpredictable accidents that lead to its reduction.

Follain asked: *'le devoir du poète n'est-il pas de tout sauver?'* ('isn't it the poet's duty to save everything?'). In his poems, he continues to make available the intense sensations that give life value, even after the disappearance of the objects or events – however insignificant – that provoked them. Although he can't return stolen property or bring back the dead, perhaps, in the way of a magistrate, he is able to offer us some form of compensation.

From Ici-bas, 1941 (*Usage du Temps*)

Woman eating almonds

The sad woman eating almonds
reaches out a hand to the still white baby
and the light down on her arms
catches some of the dust in the air.
Sitting on a stone bench
clocks strike all around her.
Swollen with shame she has known
on her body impure hands
and this wild-rose arch
is her sanctuary.
She can hear her brother arguing
near the fragile plums.
Struck by the harsh sun
her black jacket turns red;
the subdued wind has dropped.
Her strong teeth
crush the brittle almonds.
False ones gleam in every field.

Man drinking beer

He reads novels about detectives,
although he once translated Homer's epics;
he watches his glass of beer go red
in the great European sunset.
There are fumes lurking everywhere
needing release;
there are men with riddled, mangled organs,
with erupting cancers
and down some path
a dog is dying on furrowed black earth.
He drinks, slowly, this man of the North,
a very strong beer
whose bitter taste goes well with the gold of old interiors
and taking the measure of each sip
he grasps the handle of the glass
and brings it to his lips,
stained with the purple ink of schooldays
when he strutted up and down
pulling his illuminated tongue
in the July yard with its trees already brown.

Makeshift meals

To Georges Duveau

Sausage like red marble
that the labourer eats
with a sharpened knife
in a road without sky
while a baby cries
by a pewter counter!

Riot food
like those tough smoked fish
that were handed out
with raw blue wine
to pale Commune soldiers
huddled under flocks of stars.

From 'Transparence du monde', 1942–43 (*Usage du Temps*)

Before the Conception

Now the rouged boutiques light up
her skirt smells of wild skin
her heart is beating beneath her pink breasts.
It is two hours before the joyless conception
a long way from the equator
and the poles.
She is running towards the child in the darkness
in an age of ice saints
with no prophetic star
strapped into the style of a year
which shows off her thin waist.
The waiting father-to-be
tastes the lingering salt in his mouth
and wipes his lips over his wrecked plate
on which brown sauce is left
in glossy ribbon trails.

From *Territoires,* 1953 and 1969

Red Ice

In 1812 in Russia
when the soldiers beat their retreat
back through the corpses
of men and horses
their vital wine ration froze
a sapper's hatchet
then had to split
between everyone even the dying
the block of red ice
in the shape of a barrel
which no museum
could have ever preserved.

The egg

The old woman wipes an egg
on her well-worn apron
a heavy egg the colour of ivory
that no one is clamouring for
then she looks out at the autumn
through the attic window
and it's like a miniature
the same size as a picture card
there's nothing there
out of season
and the fragile egg
she's holding in her palm
is the only new thing left.

The way home

A small girl comes into the wineshop
to fetch her dad
he swears but ends up following
the pale figure with the wrought braid
leading the way
turning her head at times
to make sure he's still at her heels
this weary drunk in clagging overalls
whose wife has a smile for him
her bosom clad in a blouse of shadow.

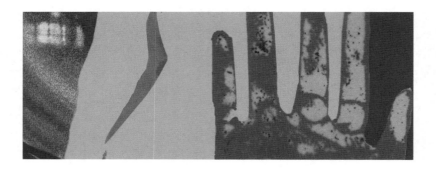

Doris Kareva
three poems
Translated by Ilmar Lehtpere

Doris Kareva was born in Tallinn, Estonia in 1958. She studied English Literature at Tartu University, and worked as the literary editor of the cultural weekly *Sirp*. She has published thirteen books of poetry, including one children's book and and two bilingual books. She has translated essays, plays and poetry into Estonian, including work by Anna Akhmatova, Emily Dickinson, Joseph Brodsky, and Shakespeare. Volumes of her poetry have been published in Russian, German, Swedish and Latvian translation. Her poetry has also appeared in anthologies and journals in fifteen other languages. She has received several literary prizes for her poetry. With the National Cultural Prize in 1993 she established, in collaboration with Huma Publishers, the Straw Stipend, which financed the publication of ten young poets. In 2003 she launched Grafiti, the next series of young Estonian poetry. Her book of poetry, *Mandragora*, was staged by Tallinn City Theatre in 2003. Her latest volume, *Aja kuju (The Shape of Time)*, which appeared in 2005, was awarded the State Cultural Prize and was chosen by Estonian Television as book of the year. She has been Secretary-General of the Estonian National Commission for UNESCO since 1992.

Läbi mu unede jooksevad kõrbekoerad,
kerged, kiired ja kuulmatud,
justnagu Jumala tuul;
kaunid ja kuninglikud, ööst öösse
nad sööstavad pöörastena.

Haistan, mõistagi haistan:
mu süda on nende saak.

Kuidas ma saaksingi tunda täiust,
kui ma ei jookseks tühjaks;
kui ma ööst öösse ei jookseks, ei kihutaks
viirastuslike, võõrastuslike
kõrbekoertega võidu.

*   *   *

Desert dogs run through my dreams,
light, swift and silent
like the winds of God;
beautiful and regal, night after night
they career headlong.

I scent, of course I scent
my heart is their prey.

How can I ever know fulfilment
if I don't deplete myself
night after night, running, racing
against the distant, spectral
desert dogs.

Skalpell ja metronoom
mu isa klaveril
enda vahel hoidsid vaikust,
kui ma olin laps.

Nüüd alles, aegamööda,
olen hakand kuulma,
mõistma
nende kummalisi lugusid.

Imeõhukeseks ihuvad need aja.

*   *   *

The scalpel and metronome
on my father's piano
kept a silence between them
when I was a child.

Only now, over time,
have I begun to hear,
to understand
their curious tales.

These whet time to a rare thinness.

Tähtede sadu tiheneb üha.

Mõni jääb kinni rinda
ja kilgendab kummastavalt.

Paat õõtsub vaevatud vetel.

Millal sa viimati märjale liivale
tõmbasid sõna,
mis elas?

*   *   *

The rain of stars grows ever heavier.

One or two are caught in the breast
and flare uncannily.

The boat rolls on unsettled waters.

When did you last pull onto wet sand
a word
that lived?

Hilde Domin
'To whom it happens'
Translated by Ruth Ingram

Hilde Domin was born in 1909 of Jewish parentage. She studied law, philosophy and politics in Heidelberg. With the advent of the Nazis, she and her husband moved to Florence where she continued her studies and obtained a doctorate. When Jews were beginning to be arrested in Italy she fled with her husband to England. By this time war had broken out, and she was regarded as an enemy alien. Nevertheless, she was given a teaching post before eventually sailing to Santo Domingo, where she and her husband both taught at the University. She adopted the name 'Domin' for all her literary writings.

After twenty-two years in exile she returned to Germany and lived in Heidelberg. She died 23 February 2006, aged 96.

Much of Hilde Domin's work is about exile and survival. 'Wen es trifft' (literally the person who has been targetted by a weapon or by fate) is a good example. Her poems have been translated into sixteen languages. She has won countless literary prizes, and has held several university posts for literature and specifically poetry. She has also written several autobiographical pieces, lectures and essays.

'Wen es trifft', here translated as 'To whom it happens', was

written in October 1953 on Maine Island just before her return
to Germany. In her autobiographical writings she mentions the
lines: 'and because it is autumn/ his blood/ shall feed the great
vines/ and make them proof against the frost'. They were
inspired by a gardener in Minehead who used animal blood as
manure, which greatly upset her.

To whom it happens

The one
to whom it happens
will be lifted up
as if by a giant crane
and put down
where nothing is valid,
where no street
leads from yesterday to tomorrow.
All buttons, jewellery and colours
will be swept from his clothes.
Then he will be stripped
and exposed.
Malevolent hands
will finger the hips.
He will be boiled under pressure
in tears
till the flesh
on the bones is soft
as in the slow kitchens of time.
He will be pressed
through the finest
sieves of pain

and will be passed
through the merciless cloths
to the last grain of identity.
So he will be selected
and punished
and must eat the dust
on all the roads of betrayal
from the soles of the disappointed,
and because it is autumn
his blood
shall feed the great vines
and make them proof
against the frost.

Sometimes, however,
if he is lucky
but through no recognizable
merit
just as he has not been selected
for a known offence
but quite simply because he was available
he will be pardoned
by the unknown
all-powerful authority
if there is still time.
Then he will be re-discovered
like a lost continent
or a crucifix
in the rubble of the cellar
after an air raid.

It is as if the points on the track
had been set:
his Nowhere is coupled
to the old landscape
as one shunts a carriage

from a siding
to a train.
Under the rainbow arch
a tender yesterday recognises him and
opens its arms to receive him
at a known date
which is heavy with future.

No cat with seven lives,
no lizard and no starfish
whose limbs grow again,
no sliced worm
is as resilient as a human
whom one lays in the sun
of love and hope.
Together with the brand marks on his body
and the scars of the wounds
his fear fades.
His bare tree of joy
grows new buds.
Even the bark of trust
grows back slowly.
He gets used to the changed
furrowed image
in the mirrors,
he oils his skin
and covers the skeleton
with a new layer of fat
till he does not smell strange
to anyone.
And quite unnoticed
perhaps on a holiday
or on a birthday
he no longer just sits on the edge
of the offered chair
as if ready for flight

or the furniture had worm-eaten legs,
but he sits with his family and friends
at the table, and is at home
and nearly safe
and is happy
with his presents
and loves what is lent
more than what is owned
and every day is for him
a surprising Here
as radiant and light
and clearly defined
as the span
between the stretched
flight feathers
of a gliding bird.

The terrible break
of the trials
subsides
like a deep between islands.
At all borders
the barriers
are moved into the light again.
But the substance
of the self
is as different
as the metal that comes out of the furnace.
Or if he had fallen
from the tenth or twentieth floor
(like a *salto mortale*
without safety net)
on to his feet
in the middle of Times Square
just missing
the jaws of the cars

before the changing red light.
But he still retains
a certain lightness
like a bird.

But you
who meet him
on every street,
you who break bread with him
stoop down and stroke
the delicate moss on the ground
without damaging it
or a little animal
so it does not recoil.
Lay your hand protectively
on the head of a child,
let it be kissed
by the tender mouth
of your lover,
or hold it
as under a tap
beneath the flowing gold
of the afternoon sun
so that it becomes transparent
and totally useless
for any part
in the erecting of
barbed wire hells
public or private
and that it never
cries 'Here'
when panic distributes its
terrible weapons
and never
gets to hold the great iron rod
that cuts through another form

as if it were foam.
And that it never
on any evening
comes home
like a hunting dog
with a pheasant
or a little hare
as instinctive prey
and puts the skin
of a You
on the table.

So that when
on the last day
it lies before you
on the bedcover
like a pale flower
so weary
but not quite so light
and not quite so pure
but like a human hand
which is stained
and will be washed
and again stained
you thank it
and say
Farewell
my hand,
you were a loving
limb
between me and the world.

Lyubomir Nikolov
three poems
Translated by Clive Wilmer and Viara Tcholakova

Chimneys

In the half-dark I observe the chimneys,
these long-extinct volcanoes. Dawn.
And exactly at the stroke of seven
high over the city bells chime.

They too are chimneys and having turned
their dusty craters to the earth
they belch into its rosy face
the heavens' polyphony.

Before my eyes a bell's peal
and wisps of smoke gradually merge
the way the wet stones merge
with their green manes of moss.

I can see the sounds. They wade through the sky
and their heels smell of sweet lava.
In secret the smoke whispers to me —
and blows away.

Translated by Clive Wilmer and the author.

A Wasp

I had only half-opened one of the window's wings...
Ovid, *Amores*

High over our bed, a wasp.

And this slim Egyptian queen
is dancing in the hot air,
spinning, vibrating in a sunbeam,
whizzing between the curtains, swooping,
circling the downy quince,
then rising again, buzzing, drifting on air,
and tracing yellow circles around the quince,
till all of a sudden the head thrusts deep
into the fruit's tunnel.

The whole body wants to squeeze into it...

Wants to get wings and sting and all
into the darkness.
To suck tart juice with the proboscis
and, sunk into the damp womb,
to dart in it like lightning,
to reach as far down as the oozy pip,
that we might hear it booming
like the Deluge with its awesome waves, and later
erupting from the darkness a limpid drop
will moisten the flattened down.

Translated by Clive Wilmer and Viara Tcholakova.

Hornets

From the hollowed heads of sunflowers
my father has made a bonfire in the garden.
And hornets, having smelt the sun,
come down upon him in their angry swarms.
He wants victory over them.
The fire keeps growing, licking the stars,
the monsters beat their wings of darkness
and the flames sting their bellies.
Some of them, almost burnt, must drag
their smoking, wingless bodies through the grass,
expiring on the damp covers
in damp sheets of dew.
Their wicked seed is wiped out almost.
My father gleefully rubs his hands
but from time to time a bee flits by
to be lost in the flames forever:
one small bee less to return to the hive...
Until morning, my father will toss in fever.
When the sun crawls up out of the earth —
the burning body of a bee.

Translated by Clive Wilmer and Viara Tcholakova.

Rilke
Four poems from the *Book of Hours*
Translated by Susan Ranson

In his *Book of Hours*, written 1899–1903, the young Rilke addresses prayers to his personal God. This is a God of contradictions: in need of humanity to perfect himself, numinous but vulnerable, gilded but work-begrimed. In 1903 Rilke had arrived in Paris; shocked at its poverty, he flies in God's face with these bitter poems. He sets God, for his self-completion, among the poor as most abject of them all and cries out to him what inhabitants of cities have always cried out.

Three of these poems express the nadir of Rilke's urban mood; 'Lord, we are poorer' mourns our failure to carve ourselves even a personal, dignified death. Immediately before this poem, Rilke visualizes urban death as a fruit hanging green within the personality, unripe because unnatural.

Rilke describes more than poverty, and even now cities vary in how they fulfil his words. Some are as wretched now as then; others, in unforeseen ways, are worse. Even the 'fine city' to which I have recently removed insidiously oppresses by its callousness and suspicion, disorder of environments and minds, unforgiving physical materials, fume and grime, alarms, sirens, haste and traffic.

Since my youth the *Book of Hours* has bound me to continue
translating it; the work is more or less complete. These last
poems only recently became familiar and astonish me by the
contrast they make with the preceding poems, no matter that
there too the guises of the divine are human and humble. Here
Rilke's verses are as insistently mellifluous as ever, but the new
desperation in their voice is loud in our ears.

Cities turn their force full on their own . . .
(Die Städte aber wollen nur das Ihre . . .)

Cities turn their force full on their own,
wrenching things along in their course: here are
animals snapped in half like hollow stems,
communities casually razed in flame.

Subservient to cult and craze, their people
tip out of balance, lapse from their mean,
count their snail-tracks an advance, hasten
where they had used to go soberly, and learn
to glitter, putting on the minds of whores,
and set their glass and metal screaming.

Day on day aped by an illusion,
they strain and fail to find real lives,
and in their eyes money rises, violent
like the east wind; and they are only small,
and held in abeyance, waiting for wine, for all
the juice of animal and human poisons
to tempt them towards the transient.

And these your poor linger, weak from poison . . .
(Und deine Armen leiden unter diesen . . .)

And these your poor linger, weak from poison
and bent under the brunt of what they see;
they walk in fierce sweats like fever-chill,
by night aimless as ghosts of refugees
turned from house after house; laden with dirt
that heaps about them; spat on like putrefaction
under the sun – and targeted by the shrill
yell from dolled prostitutes, and the scream
of lights, vehicles, and of the accidental.

If there be any mouth for their protection
stir it to speech, to the responsible.

Bear them away again from urban corruption . . .
(Nur nimm sie wieder aus der Städte Schuld . . .)

Bear them away again from urban corruption:
from the disturbed and angry environs wasting
their substance; from tumultuous existence
wounding, despite all, their brave patience.

Has the earth no place for them? Whom does the thrill
of the wind seek? Who drinks of the brook's brilliance?
And in the deep of the pond's reverie
is there no space to reflect their door, their sill?
The poor, as we know, need only a small niche
in which to build their whole world, like a tree.

Lord, we are poorer than the poor beasts . . . (Herr: Wir sind ärmer denn die armen Tiere . . .)

Lord, we are poorer than the poor beasts,
which end at their death. They too die blind,
but we have all less than entirely died.
Give us the man who wins the precious skill
to bind life in espaliers, which guide
maturing May sooner to the autumnal.

Dying is difficult and alien
for this: it is not *ours* but takes us
because we cannot bring our own to ripen.
So, in a storm, it strips us from the branches.

We stand, Lord, year on year in your garden,
your trees for nurturing a sweet death;
but by the harvest we have grown sere,
and like the woman you have struck barren
find ourselves closed, false to our promise, fruitless.

Or is my arrogance too much? Are trees
in the end better? Are we only womb
and sex of women who yield all too freely?
For we can be said to whore with eternity,
and when we come to childbed bring forth
only the stillborn foetus of our death:
embryo, bent, full of misery,

trying to cover with its mere hands
(as though in fear of the fearful) eyes unformed
still; and on its bulged forehead stands
dread of all it has not suffered under –
so die we all, like just so many whores,
in labour pains; from caesareans.

Amina Saïd
four poems
Translated by Marilyn Hacker

Amina Saïd was born in Tunisia in 1952, and now lives in Paris. She is the author of eight collections of poetry, most recently *De Décembre à la mer* (2001) and *La Douleur des seuils* (2003), with a ninth forthcoming this year. She has also published two books of tales and fables from Tunisia, and several translations of novels by the Filipino writer F. Sionil José. Poems of hers, in my translation, have appeared in the American journals *Rattapallax, Prairie Schooner* and *The Manhattan Review*.

Blood of the Sea

1.
Djibouti
unstable star
beneath the moon's capsized arc

Djibouti
crossroads of dust

naked children play
on the shore of the Red Sea

time's shepherd man
looks towards the desert's eternity

we are the pilgrims of errancy
says the poet

2.
secret network of trails

shadow of stones at prayer
sacred circle
for chattering saints
stones upon stones
stones for life
stones for death

3.
the ancestors watch over
the children of Dammerjog
a goat meditates in the courtyard
the bird weaves its nest on the tree of sky

4.
what have you come to do in my country
says the tale of the schoolboy from Boulaous
and what are you looking for?

5.
Maskali
white boat
come to meet an island dream
buttressed on the sea's passion
where am I if there's nothing but a horizon-line?

we approach the sandy cove
the trees here are made of coral

6.
canyon chasm inhabited by djinns
echoing the dark
of my childhood nightmares

7.
Goubet el-Kharâb cones of desolation
twin breasts
bathed by the sea's blood

8.
stones upon stones
stones darkened by all the world's sins

stones scattered on the earth's fire
ambergris pearls of the divine rosary

stones to the right
stones to the left
stones for life
stones for death
hell and heaven have no borders

9.
camels goats gazelles
like a sign above us
a hawk breaches space

a few trees implore the cloud's whiteness
a condensation of tears
as many prayers gone up in smoke

10.
gash, knife-wound, scar
in the mineral flesh
yawning gap in the fault
view of the abyss

11.
wide-open eye beneath a shroud of salt
Lake Assal pins the sun at zenith

crystals of pure light
caravans petrified as the world ages

saline waters of burning bitterness
virgin waters liquid veins

who struck the stone
so that the source gushed forth?

12.
brute stones free stones
black and ochre pawns on the giant chessboard
stumps in the earth's toothless laughter
Satan's landmarks
there are no happy stones

13.
barbed memory
gripping the bronze soil

line of demarcation
rampart of thorns played with by the wind

the nomads have entered the city

14.
beneath the poet's portrait
the child from Hadj-Diddeh asks me
did you know Rimbaud, ma'am?

on the seventh day of my birth
I spoke the language
of the world I'd come from
bore witness to a shadow
which was the shadow
of another light
which no one saw

in the seventh month of my birth
my mouth took the shape of the void
I cried to tell what was true
and that which the present had taught me
of the past of the future
but no one understood

the seventh year of my birth
I dreamed what had been
on the world's lined page
I traced letter after letter
to remind myself
of what I had to forget
and of what in me was already dying

I was ten years old head full of sky
I borrowed the sun's wings
to fly toward that spot between two shores

I built towers of sand
where that shadow lived which served as my body

body ripened by a sun of extreme summer
I was in the wind's thoughts
intonations of light
composed my landscape

I was ten years old in the colour of day
I scowled with the stones
where scorpions sheltered
on the island, women went masked
perhaps out of modesty

sky in my head I would make myself invisible
to see better knocked at windowpanes
where the day gathered
in an ordinary hymn
I looked for meaning in form—
somewhere out there the world had to exist

I was twenty years old impatient
to shore up at new continents
I left my father's house
gave my avian liberty up to the light
entered the space of darkness

I tried to open invisible doors
claimed to read the very stuff of silence
like a mother tongue
made a beginning of the past
and a double absence of the present

body more alive than dead
I refused to let night separate me
from day or day from night

watcher of dreams whom a dream invented
what was I looking for when I opened my eyes
on the colours of the world
which the sun never lets out of its sight

from words' second memory
real feeling is born
I inhabit that music
which I can't be the only one to hear

shadow which follows or precedes its shadow
on the border between dream and real
I stay on my own margins
in space and time

how to know if in this nowhere
place where a voice sets itself free
I came of my own free will
or if it was imposed on me

I was that other
in the exhilaration of unsettled wandering
in a time when dressed with pure water and sleek suns
I was still growing on a real earth
in a time when I expected everything of dawn
of immortal night of day's enchantment
of my twin in blood and words
of a time when our encounters
were always the first
in a time when separated from myself
I loved with unclairvoyant impatience
in a time when I guessed before I understood
diluted myself in forgotten gardens
in a time when life did not imagine itself other
when I claimed a spot
in the world's bright nakedness
when my blood beat in the poem's veins
when silence preceded words
lending them its vision of a time when words
were rootless birds
birds of passion in a sky heavy with waiting
dropping as in a dream at dusk
in a time when I dreamed with my eyes open
when I persisted between the visible and the invisible
when I searched for the greatest light
in a time when death had not been invented

twilight woman
drawing a gift of words from the well of nothing
I was every age now I am none
I left a body's imprint
on the cracked night of cities
only a stopping-point with no assuagement
twilight woman given up to the flaws
in the shadow of the mask behind faces

absence is measured by the blue of silence
time draws new frontiers for me
the inner shadow is cast
on the salt of the page

I need a time of rupture
so the wandering can continue

Jeff Nosbaum
versions from the *Aeneid* and the *Iliad*

'That only one would not make landfall', from the *Aeneid*, Book V.

Note

The story of Palinurus' fate is preceded by Aeneas' visit to the oracle of Neptune. Here, Neptune promises Aeneas that he and all his followers except one will finally be allowed to reach their destination. However, the oracle does not reveal to Aeneas who the unlucky one will be, and Aeneas, in his joy at Neptune's promise, barely notices the caveat. Book V then ends with the only passage of sustained focus Palinurus receives in the Aeneid. Despite this brevity of appearance, there is a lyrical quality to the passage that fixes Palinurus in the mind, and I wrote this version out of a desire to intensify that quality by giving Palinurus a poem of his own.

Then down came Sleep from Heaven, adrift
on the night, like a passing breeze in search of peace:
so Sleep sought Palinurus, almost playful; and
the demigod sat upon the deck, spoke
to the guiltless helmsman, saying 'Father, this sea
is a mirror in the dark, smooth, unbroken
even by reflection, and the night is clear
as might the Lord of Heaven grant Himself
were we to be so honoured, please – ' and raised
his hand for the tiller, but Palinurus
did not stir, his eyes did not turn from the fore,
his grip never lessened, and so again,
'Father, hear me: Sleep's hour has arrived.
Lay your head upon the deck and close
your eyes, I'll guide the fleet till dawn – '
but Palinurus neither stirred, nor did
he shift his grip, his eyes remaining wide
and fixed upon the sea before them, so that
inwardly, the god seethed: for he was Sleep
and like Hunger, Death, no man denied him,
but smooth and youthful was the face that smiled
as Palinurus' second rose, and dove,
a dolphin now, into the sea, pulling Palinurus
to his feet to peer down at the god
glistening in the dark, whose eyes engulfed
the peerless helmsman so that he fell
(though it felt like rising) into the water,
and the sea was soon a mirror and the night
a bell, vast above him as he breathed
his last, and the fleet bore onward, guided
by the sea, Neptune mindful of his promise.

'The Fall of Troy'

Note

This is a loose version written from memory. In the original,
Apollo attacks Patroclus before Hector does, making Hector's
defeat of Patroclus less a matter of a greater warrior defeating a
lesser warrior than of Hector merely finishing the job Apollo
has begun. Apollo's attack also knocks Achilles' helmet off
Patroclus, revealing his true identity to Hector. I thought it
would be interesting to remove Apollo from the scene, both to
intensify the encounter between Patroclus and Hector and in
order to leave Hector's awareness that he is not fighting
Achilles an innate sense rather than a revealed fact.

The first clash of sword and shield
turned white the gold-hued
flesh of the shieldbearer's forearm,
reverberated
up through his shoulder and
out across his torso like a lightning
strike about a heart that beat now quite
alone. The field fell away
from Patroclus, pinned
within Hector's event horizon.
As the horsebreaker's arm drew back
for the second stroke, Achilles' cousin knew
today, he would be dead
but bent his knee as brace
beneath the blow. If the first was lightning, this,
an earthquake, shook him witless:
arms fell limp, shield spun useless in
the dust, and he kneeled
before what seemed to be a god aglow with power.

Hector steps back and sheathes his sword.
He hefts the spear above his head and meets
the eyes of one he thinks Achilles and
somehow, in that moment, knows,
but still he throws with the force
he will require for Thetis' son;
and the spear pierces
the breastplate of Achilles
and then Patroclus' breast.

Hsieh Ling-yün
'By the Stream'
Translated by Alastair Thomson via the Spanish of Octavio Paz

Octavio Paz (1914–1998) is one of the greatest Latin American poets of our time. Born in Mexico City, he worked in several countries, including India, where he was Mexican Ambassador, resigning in 1968 after the Mexico City massacre of student demonstrators. Paz translated widely, from Japanese, English, French, Portuguese, Swedish, Chinese, and Sanskrit. In 1990 he was awarded, tardily enough, the Nobel Prize for Literature. He describes Hsieh Ling-yün (385–433) as sometimes a potentate, sometimes a hermit, both revolutionary politician and sybarite, painter by affection, poet by fate, and describes this particular poem as a dialogue between two lovers, both married.

Por el arroyo

— ¡Qué raro, qué lindo!
La esposa de alguno
en el agua obscura
lava sus pies blancos.

Entre nubarrones
relumbra la luna,
tan lejos, tan lejos
que nadie la alcanza.

— ¡Qué lindo, qué raro!
De alguna el esposo
por el río obscuro
pasa en blanca barca.

Iba a preguntarle
qué se le ofrecía
pero entre las nubes
se escondió la luna.

By the Stream

— How rare, how lovely!
Someone's wife
In the dark water washes
Her white feet.

Among storm clouds
Shines the moon,
So far, so far
No one may reach it.

— How lovely, how rare!
On the dark river
Someone's husband goes by
In a white boat.

I was going to ask him
What he had in mind,
But the moon hid herself
Among the clouds.

Yu Xuanji
two poems
Translated by Justin Hill

Yu Xuanji (830–856) is China's foremost female poet, who lived during the last years of the Tang Dynasty (618-907). She was married at sixteen as a concubine; divorced when she was nineteen, and after a time spent as a Daoist nun and courtesan, she was executed at the age of twenty-six, after murdering her maid.

Convention set passive roles for women in poetry: but Yu Xuanji flouted these – with many of her poems attacking limitations set on women and protesting at the cultural norms which said that a woman's beauty peaked in mid-teens. Her social defiance and the manner of her death meant that most of her poems were lost, but forty-nine were collected in the Song Dynasty, mainly for their curiosity-value in an anthology which also listed poems by ghosts, monks, priests, foreigners and women 'and others whose efforts might provide amusement'.

Visiting Abbot Zhao Lianshi and finding him not in

Wandering with the immortals,
only his green coat is at home.

Medicine simmers on the stove,
in the side yard I sit and boil some tea.

On the painted wall the lamp is unlit,
while the flag pole's shadow slants in the sunlight.

Turning home, I keep looking over my shoulder:
to enjoy the sight of trees in blossom by his gate.

By the Yangtse River

I
Our boat slants across the wide river
to Wuchang City
past Parrot Island
home to ten thousand households,
in the painted pleasure boat
lovers sleep in the early morning
and I dream myself a butterfly
searching for a flower.

II
Mist's rising and we're sailing
into Cormorant Port.
I thought we were out
near Parrot Island
where I lay down drunk
and sang my heart out —
then I woke amazed to find myself
here on the Hanjiang side.

Kaneko Misuzu
four poems
translated by Quentin Crisp

Kaneko Misuzu (née Teru) was born on 11 April, 1903, in Yamaguchi Prefecture. Her hometown of Senzaki was a fishing village, overlooking the Sea of Japan. At the time when Teru was growing up the town was alive with the stir and bustle of fishermen, and sometimes the entire town would assist the fishing fleet in bringing ashore a large haul.

In 1924, Kaneko Teru ('Kaneko' is the family and 'Teru' the given name) adopted the pen name 'Misuzu' and sent her first poems to magazines such as *Golden Star* (*Kin no Hoshi*), *Stories for Children* (*Dowa*) and *Housewives' Club* (*Fujin Kurabu*).

In 1927 she entered into an arranged marriage, which proved unhappy for her. Her husband forbade her to write poetry or continue correspondence with her friends and associates from the magazines. She found consolation, however, in her baby daughter.

Her husband brought her further unhappiness by spending long periods away from home, frequenting the pleasure quarters, and even passing on to her a disease he had caught there. In 1930, she asked for a divorce with the single condition that she could keep her daughter. Her husband agreed, but soon changed his mind about custody of the child.

As a divorced woman, at that time, Teru had no legal rights to the child. When her husband asked for custody and eventually said he was coming in person to take the child, Teru felt that her only recourse was a protest suicide. She asked, in one note, for her mother to look after the child, and in another she asked her husband to allow this. On 9 March, 1930, she took an overdose. She was twenty-six years old.

Although popular in her lifetime, and compared by one enthusiastic editor to Christina Rossetti, after her death she was forgotten until her recent rediscovery in Japan about ten years ago. Her cosmic view of nature has a new resonance in the 21st century with the growing awareness of the importance of the environment beyond its immediate utility and of the interconnectedness of things.

Night Harbour

A cloudy night.
Trembling, trembling, tiny,
One star.

Such a cold night.
From the boat, reflecting in the rocking waves,
Two lights.

A lonely night.
Shining blue from the ocean,
Three little eyes.

Waves

The waves are children.
They hold hands and laughing
Race towards you in a line.

The waves are an eraser.
The letters written in the sand
Are all erased by them.

The waves are soldiers.
In from the offing they march
And together fire a volley from their rifles.

The waves are always forgetting things.
Such pretty, pretty shells
Left behind on the sand.

Things not Seen

What happened while you slept?

Pale pink petals fell
As rain in heaps on your bed.
You opened your eyes and they vanished.

Nobody ever saw them,
But who can say it's a lie?

What happened when you blinked?

down of an empty form, here and ever again leads to weightless beauty without a first or second name.

It is the wardrobe mistress, then, who reserves the right to call out a Vera or Tasha to this now perspiring twenty-seven-year-old creature, to see a body marked by hard labour that lisps and no longer has an appendix. Now it becomes apparent how harmlessly and tritely the break between two gracefully strenuous peak performances can be spent. The ballerina knits woollen socks for her little brother; the ballerina chatters brainlessly, the ballerina has recently got engaged, though it isn't at all impossible that she will soon disengage herself. The ballerina puts on a pair of glasses, she is a bit short-sighted and flicks through an illustrated magazine, till she's found the crossword puzzle and solved half of it. Now the ballerina weeps a little. Her balance was not good today, she 'wobbled the arabesque' and in the third pirouette she 'slipped off her points' – and she must not do that.

The tenor may grope for the chair's back, as long as he sings. Lizzy may stagger a bit in the midst of the waltz and remark profoundly that everything is turning anyway. No one will be angry with her about that. Only when the ballerina 'slips off her points' the front stalls freeze, then it grows hot in the back stalls, the stage expands, day-bright and sober, programmes are folded, opened, and all the whispering denotes that the ballerina is all of twenty-seven, lisps and no longer has an appendix.

Of Dancing Barefoot

The ballerina's enemy and deadly serious opposite is the expressive dancer. While the ballerina moves her body according to rigid rules and smiles in the act, as though indifference had been painted into the corners of her mouth, the expressive dancer dances with her difficult psyche and moves her limbs accordingly, as though her private knee, crooked at that, were reason enough to fascinate one eighth of the front stalls and the half-full back stalls for two hours. The ballerina lives at her mother's, does not smoke, eats yoghurt and bananas, feeds a little dog and before and after training feels tired, never anything but tired.

The expressive dancer is cultured. She can recite the 'lay of love and death' by heart and has seen Cocteau's *Orphée* five times. In her furnished room hangs an African mask, a Paul Klee print and the photograph of a Malayan temple dancer. She makes her own clothes and never carries her long, beautiful hair to the hairdresser's. Because the ballerina goes to bed early, her night life, apart from a few visits to the cinema, is regulated in a very innocent way. The expressive dancer has a pianist boy friend. Both live in constant fear of a baby, but long for a baby, she for a string of children, motherhood. Now, to make up for that, with her hair loose – hence her avoidance of the hairdresser – in a sack-like garment she dances lullabies, expectations, releases – her most recent creation has the title Weeping Embryo.

The expressive dancer dances barefoot, that's why she could be called a barefoot dancer. The ballerina's exercise is like a monotonous Prussian discipline. Her tormented, constricted flesh hides behind white, red, even silver ballet shoes. The ballerina's feet can be described as ugly. Scraped, open toes, enlarged bridges. They seem to be the true sacrifice of all this validly exhibited beauty. Down there all that collects which, above, is concealed by harmonious gestures and the bland smile. The measure of these shoes goes back to the Middle Ages and the Inquisition. So we may take the desirable thirty-two *fouettés* to be a confession, and nothing, no barefoot dance, will be able to replace this confession, this penance.

Asceticism in Front of the Mirror

The ballerina, like a nun, lives exposed to every temptation, in a state of the strictest asceticism. This analogy should not surprise you, since all the art come down to us has been the product of consistent restriction, never the immoderation of genius. Even if at times breakouts into the impermissible made and make us think that all is permitted in art, always even the most mobile of minds invented rules for itself, fences, forbidden rooms. So too our ballerina's room is restricted, surveyable, and permits changes only within the area available to her. The demands of the age will always require the ballerina to put on a new face, will hold exotic or pseudo-exotic masks in front of it. She will join in that decorative little game, knowing that every fashion suits her. The true revolution, though, will have to take place in her own palace.

How similar it is in painting. How meaningless seem all attempts to see fundamental discoveries in the invention of new materials, in exchanging oil painting for a process of lacquer sprayed on to aluminium. Never will dilettantism, easily recognizable by its mannerisms, drive out the pertinacious flow of the skill that remains conservative even in its revolutions.

The ballerina turns mirrors into the least indulgent implement of asceticism. Wide awake she trains in front of their surface. Her dance is not the dance with closed eyes. Mirrors to her are nothing more than a glass that throws everything back, with exaggerated clarity, merciless moralists she is commanded to believe. What liberties a poet takes with mirrors. What mystical, illegible postcards he drops into their baroque frames. To him mirrors are an exit, entrance, he searches like a still ignorant kitten behind the pane and, at best, finds a broken little box there, filled with buttons that do not match, a bundle of old letters he never expected to find again, and a comb full of hairs. Only at moments of irreversible transformation, when our bodies seem enriched or impoverished, do we stand in front of mirrors as she does, with eyes as awake. Mirrors show girls their puberty, no pregnancy escapes them, no missing tooth – should laughter try to provoke them. Perhaps a hairdresser, a taxi driver, a tailor, a painter at his self-portrait, a prostitute who has furnished her little room with a number of these clarifying shards, have something in common with the ballerina. It is the anxious gaze of the craftsman, of a person who works with his or her body, it is a gaze into the confession glass.

Applause and Curtains

Applause is the ballerina's small cash. She counts it very carefully, and if these coins, like other hard cash, could be kept in a stocking, she would save them up for later days, when there will be a shortage of hands, no one will be moved to clap, and clapping could hurt, because the man in charge of the curtain will have no more reason to make strokes on a little board, till this means: sixteen curtains tonight, two more than last night.

The ballerina shows the same thoroughness and meticulousness with which we count the cuckoo's calls on a Sunday walk through the city park, when it's a matter of deducing the number of possible curtains from the duration and density of the applause. She counts and wishes to tempt the front and back stalls with her precise and graceful acknowledgements, as we tempt the cuckoo that calls out the number of our years. Then, after the last curtain, the ballerina collapses like a house of cards suddenly exposed to the wind. Each of her limbs, otherwise so poised, slides into anything goes. The order on her face, on this plate full of cosmetic delicacies, relaxes. Her eyes are not up to a single glance, over-taxed they lose their grip and widen alarmingly. Her mouth likewise. Always ready to burst into hysteria, now a smile, meant kindly, becomes so great an exertion for it that a cramp threatens its corners. What's it for, this constant wrinkling of the forehead, this raising of the eyebrows? Every constituent of the performance put on with so much effort and accomplishment now leaves its place. The ballerina seems completely out of hand.

The Little Point

She raises a slightly limp arm. At the top the hand
materializes, a useless, many-limbed continuation. All this
with no meaning, fit only for looking at, not even a greeting or
an invitation to come closer. Half-way to being an ornament, it
serves only to show what's there, that an arm bends there and
divides the background, that in the direction of the little finger
there is a little point which all beauty obeys – and so does the
ballerina. Never does it occur to her that the arm could be
bent differently, bent so as to convey only power, desperation
or, disagreeably crooked, a mere accident. Never she would
direct her finger to any point but this one, which is
meaningless as a goldfinch and yet so spacious, so insatiable
that all our ballast could get lost in it. For if we were to say to
our ballerina, 'Oh, why don't you dance the atom bomb
for us!', she would turn seven pirouettes and them come to a
halt, smiling. And if someone came along asking for traffic
problems or reunification to be danced, at once she'd show him
that combination of aesthetic figures at whose end an arabesque
achieves reunification and solves the traffic problem, by
indicating the little point.

All these demonstrations are accompanied by the 'Turkish
March' or an extract from the *Nutcracker Suite*, it makes no
difference, the ballerina isn't necessarily what one calls musical.
She lets the pianist announce, explain, count out the rhythms
and entrusts herself with exemplary credulity to the ballet
master, so that he can determine the number and sequence of
the postures, turns, *relevés*, and control her whole performance.

It can be the 'Radetzky March', too, whose inescapable
beat accompanies her course across the stage with baffling
irrelevance, if only at the end, with the last note and drumbeat,
the finger indicates that little point again, for that is right and
proper.

Nature and Art

Back once more to the little picture. The ballerina, in stiff,
easily creased material, was dancing on the table. The open
window intimated that entrance and exit demanded no door.
Easily the room, table and window can be transformed into
stage, podium, wings. The poet, a little narrow-chested on the
engraving, is also transmuted, turns into a leaping, dancing
troubadour. In a *pas de deux* the story finds its continuation.
Love, separation, temptation, jealousy and death. This plot is
simple, a mere pretext for showing the ballerina in her difficult
existence, dancing on points. In the most elaborate décor it is
the fulfilment of what daily exercise to the sound of an
out-of-tune piano prescribes for the body and the body alone.

Who forces the ballerina, this sensitive creature almost a
little insipid in her every-day life, to take her pleasure at the
bars and, under supervision of an elderly, often rather cynical
ballet mistress, to train year after year? Is it only ambition,
only a craving for success? – Reluctantly she enters the training
room, looks for her place. Reluctantly she goes through the
first motions. And then it takes hold of her. Suddenly this
battle against the body fascinates her, much as a deadly serious
march-past in slow time fascinates a declared pacifist. If it's a
stale joke to send off the poet with the too well-meant advice
always to write quite naturally, how much more unbearable for
the delicate eye would be the dancer who, at the prompting of
whatever urge, dared to skip across the stage naturally, that is,
without any decency, ebullient and lush as the vegetation in a
jungle or mere hothouse.

It has become second nature to us not to devour a piece of
mutton in its raw, still bloody state. No, we roast, boil or
steam it, always add some spice to it, call it done and palatable
at the end, eat it well-manneredly with knife and fork, a
napkin on our laps or round our necks. So the other arts ought
at last to be honoured in the same way as the culinary art and
– if now and then voices are raised and call the classical ballet

dead — we should declare admiringly that until now this art, even more than the culinary or than painting, deserves to be called the most unnatural and therefore the most formally perfect of all the arts.

Not until it has proved possible to crystallize formalities as strong as those dance movements from all experiments — and only experiments have been shown so far — formulas that like the ballet exclude anything fortuitous, will the ballerina take her last bow.

Perhaps then the man or woman-sized, wholly artificial puppet will appear. In his little treatise on the puppet theatre Kleist pointed that way, Kokoschka allowed an insensitive girl of that kind to make dresses, in Schlemmer's Triadic Ballet boldly designed figurines took the first important step. Perhaps the two will be reconciled and enter into a marriage, the marionette and the ballerina. —

Robert Hull
'One good translation deserves another'

A line sailed back into mind recently, after several years'
absence: 'Now autumn mars the green of hills, my gentle
beasts.'

I couldn't at first recall where it came from. But in a
moment or so I found it in my Penguin Modern European
Poets Quasimodo, translated by Jack Bevan in 1965, bought
not long after. Other haunting lines in the same book were
close to the surface of the memory: 'The wind is still there that
I remember / kindling the manes of horses . . .' and 'In the
spaces of the hills /all winter, the silence /of the light of sailing
ships.'

These translated lines bedded down long ago in the
same way as did memorable lines from Wordsworth, George
Herbert, Elizabeth Bishop and all the others. That they were
translated was a feature that the memory overlooked in the
pleasure of their possession as lines of poetry in English, and
irrespective of their 'quality as translation'. Only later did I
turn to the original, wondering if the Edward Hicks-ish
resonances of the line were authentic. I'm still not sure.

When Lowell's *Imitations* came out, I read it as poetry in
English – without checking, for instance, whether the lines of
Valéry's original *Helen* were as haunting as: 'I come from the

lower world/ to hear the serene erosion of the surf; / once more I see the galleys bleed with dawn / and shark with muffled rowlocks into Troy.' That incurious habit was part of the general excitement of finding so much that was newly, or freshly brought into the English.

For whole readerships too, when particular translations become integral parts of our experience as readers, either the original need not be present to the mind at all, or the need for it may fade. The literary success of a translation may mask the very existence of the original. We may forget that Yeats' 'When I am old and grey . . .' is – or was once – a translation. The King James Bible, Pound's Rihaku, Miguel Leon-Portilla's Aztec songs, Milosz's Herbert, Milner's and Theiner's Holub, Ulli Beier's Yoruba hunter-poems, and so on have in greater or lesser measure transcended their translatedness. For most readers, they have become originals themselves.

The experience of subsequently encountering alternative and plural translations may then, however, disturb such un-questioning acceptance. Reading the Akhmatova versions in *MPT* 3.3 – including two of the Dante poem – sent me back to Richard McKane's durable renderings, in the Bloodaxe *Collected Akhmatova* and in Weissbort's Penguin *Post-War Russian Poetry*. Comparing them, however, was a merely 'literary' activity, since I know no Russian.

Which is not to undervalue such essential activity. Having two or three versions to compare is usually very illuminating, can even be potentially subversive, not least when the cultural success of one version carries definitiveness or the apparent finality of implying *No translation beyond this point*. It is also valuable, on the other hand, when such comparison results in this seeming-finality being endorsed or celebrated afresh – however provisionally. Benson Bobrick's *The Making of the English Bible* (Phoenix, 2001) has some fascinating examples of those creative leaps in the process of translation which eventually, precariously, gave us the Authorised Version. Interestingly, the successes of that version were often, Bobrick

makes clear, the outcomes of decades of tinkering. Here are two
examples:

'How are the mighty overthrown', **Tyndale** *1530.*
'How are the mighty fallen', *King James Authorised Version
1611.*

'Hast thou given the horse strength? Or covered his neck with
neighing?', *Geneva Bible 1560.*
'Hast thou given the horse strength? hast thou clothed his neck
with thunder?' *AV*

Some, though, were last-minute inspirations:

'Faith is a most sure warrant of things, is a being of things
hoped for, a discovery, a demonstration that things are not
seen.'
'Now faith is the substance of things hoped for, the evidence of
things not seen.'
A V – two final options.

All three 'simple'-seeming changes – made by collaborative
committee endeavour, fascinatingly enough – are revelatory,
the first two in their directness and metaphoric clarity, the
third for its newly-found rhythmic assurance. In these ways
they – and the illumination they give to the moments of
inspiration in writing – can be compared with the extraordinary, clinching revisions Hardy made to the last lines of
stanzas of 'During Wind And Rain'.

Early version	Final version
The sickened leaves drop down in throngs	How the sick leaves reel down in throngs!
And the wind-whipt creeper lets go the wall.	And the rotten rose is ript from the wall.
On their chiselled names the lichen grows.	Down their carved names the rain-drop ploughs.

Such examples are testimony to the precariousness of all writing, but more pertinently here, underscore the truth that translating poems is no less or more than writing poetry. The poet's choices, as between this and that word, rhythmic pulse, turn of phrase, syntactical gesture, sentence length, and so on, are those the translator makes. Translations can be compared not just with drafts, but as drafts. Herein lies, then, the indispensable value of a literary scrutiny of differing versions. Take these two versions of a well-known poem by Praxilla, from fifth-century BC Greece.

Loveliest of what I leave behind is the sunlight,
And loveliest after that the shining stars, and the moon's face,
But also cucumbers that are ripe, and pears, and apples.
                                                    Trans. Richmond Lattimore

Most beautiful of things I leave is sunlight;
Then come glazing stars and the moon's face;
Then ripe cucumbers and apples and pears.   **Trans. Willis Barnstone**

Lattimore's musically greater expansiveness is, arguably, truer to the pace of the emotion of relishing things. He risks 'the's' and 'and's' to create space between each loved thing; reference becomes momentary contemplation. In the second line he repeats 'loveliest' and only arrives at 'stars' on the fifth stress of seven. He draws out the third line in an adjectival clause longer than sense requires, marking it with a couple of commas like road-humps. Barnstone's version by contrast is brisk. He takes musically and syntactically briefer options each time – as in the impatient 'then's'. His version hurries, I'd say, and sounds cramped.

This, though, is to look at two versions as only, or primarily, poems in English. I don't know Ancient Greek, and if for some reason which I can't imagine, Praxilla's poem actually sounded brisk in Ancient Greek, I suppose Barnstone would have done the better rhythmic job. But insofar as an unawareness of the original language is most readers' reason for reading a translation, they can only go on their own sense of the poetic rightness of the translation as a would-be-poem in itself. They have nothing else to go by. So I prefer Lattimore.

In the same way, William Soutar's version of the first stanza of an old Irish poem seems more elegiacally end-of-summer than Flann O'Brien's:

> Summer is by;
> There is nae mair to tell.
> Stark on the brae the stags bell:
> The drift blaws oot o' the sky:
> Summer is by.   **From the Irish – William Soutar**

> Here's a song
> stags give tongue
> winter snows
> summer goes.   **Flann O' Brien**

And two versions, both in Penguin, of Osip Mandelstam's 'The Stalin Epigram' are so different they can't help raise questions of preference. Here are a few lines side by side.

Penguin – trans. Clarence Brown and W S Merwin	**Penguin – trans. James Greene**
Our lives no longer feel ground under them.	We exist, without sensing our country beneath us,
At ten paces you can't hear our words . . .	Ten steps away our words evaporate....
the ten thick worms his fingers,	His fat fingers slimy as worms . . .
the huge laughing cockroaches on his top lip . . .	His cockroach moustache chuckles . . .
He pokes out a finger and he alone goes boom.	He alone prods and probes . . .

The concrete immediacy of Brown and Merwin dictates my preference from the first line. Subsequent lines confirm it, as in the punching rhythm of 'ten thick worms his fingers' compared with the flaccid 'fat fingers slimy as worms'; and the finger that doesn't just prod and probe but 'goes boom'.

There must surely be some legitimacy in reading like this, with an exclusive regard, as it frequently seems to be, to the literary quality of the translated poem-as-poem in English. How else can one engage with a poem from a language one doesn't know? And yet, if we are to 'return to the original', there needs also to be available the kind of translation that keeps the original language in mind and at hand. Seamus Heaney remarks about Thomas Kinsella, that his translations of *The Poems of the Dispossessed* 'are not asking to be taken as alternatives to the originals, but are offered as paths to lead our eyes left across the page, back to the Irish'; hence 'the refusal of rhyme and the disdain of a charming tune'.

So though the idea of the 'better' translation most often points – in most published works – towards the pole of the literary version, it also turns, Janus-faced, to the literal pole, the more 'faithful' rendering which guides or goads the reader towards the original. Readers for whom this pragmatic rationale for translation is more pressing, who want to be sent to original texts, will value, as the dominant criterion of translation quality, 'fidelity to the original'. Not knowing Ancient Greek or Russian, I can't be sure, according to this criterion, that Barnstone's version of Praxilla's poem isn't better than Lattimore's, James Greene's handling of the 'Stalin Epigram' more 'Mandelstam' than Brown's and Merwin's.

There's clearly a tension between these divergent aims of translation. Is it reconcilable? Towards the end of his Introduction to *The Penguin Book of Modern Verse Translation* (1966), George Steiner suggests that the 'only completely honest format' for his book would have been to have had the original on the facing page, with a prose paraphrase bracketing the principal difficulties, in the margin. He regretfully adduces reasons (like 'size, economy') why this ideal didn't seem possible, but suggests nonetheless that his anthology would 'defeat itself if it did not . . . return the reader to the original'.

Many poets, particularly, will want to know what the translated poem sounds like in the original, knowing that its music is, in part, the poem. Over the last year or two, reading modern Greek poems, particularly Seferis in Keeley and Sherrard's translation and Ritsos in both Keeley's and Pilitsis', I more and more found I needed the Greek on the opposite page, so as to hear the poems in Greek, or try to, to hear the poet's music. That way, with perhaps a dictionary and a grammar for company, one can be alerted to slippages like – here for instance – a smoothing out of syntax and rhythm:

Γεροντισσα, τιφλι, καθοταν στο κατωφλι,
μπροσ στο δρομο.
A blind old woman was sitting on her doorstep
facing the street.   **Yannis Ritsos,**
                                       trans. George Pilitsis

The aspiration to 'return' to the original may be frustrated, by the poem's origin in a script or syllabary inaccessible to the reader, the sheer effort needed to begin to read any language in the original, and so on. Too often, also, there is an original only for the translator, and even then only if the translator is as much at home in the language being translated as a native speaker. If the translator is working on a collaborator's 'literal' or 'trot', as Graves called it, then the (second) translator is as reliant on the primary literal as any other reader. With what consequences the reader cannot know. Janos Csokits says of Hughes' translations of Pilinsky, that 'without the softening effect of the original metre and rhyme-scheme they sound harsher' than in Hungarian, so in Hughes' versions 'Pilinsky's view of the world appears grimmer'. Which is the opposite effect from that noted by Heaney in overly mellifluous translations from Irish by writers like Lord Longford and Frank O'Connor. Such insights raise doubts: can Waley be trusted after all, however much (literary) pleasure he gives?
Suppose, then, that we wish to 'return to the original', how

do we do it? By learning a language and getting on with it? Then how much returning can we do? I'd ask also whether publishing has a role to perform. Following Steiner's hint, is there not much to be said for having all three manifestations of the poem – original, literal and literary versions – seen together? I value the moments in *MPT*, as elsewhere, where original and translation appear side by side. I also like the format of the old Penguin Italian, French, Spanish etc. collections, which have a prose paraphrase at the foot of the page, with the originals filling the top three-quarters. Much published poetry in translation now offers less than this, offers frequently only the one literary version. It seems there might even be a shift towards English-only translations and away from dual-language editions. The Keeley-Sherrard dual-language Seferis, for instance, appears to have given way to an English-only edition.

An argument for a plurality not just of translations but of the contexts of their appearance in publications amounts to an aggressive form of defence of the idea of translation. Scepticism as to the possibilities of translation is a constant, and perhaps easily underemphasised. It may well lie behind the incurious-ness still, in schools for instance, of our cultural relations with other literatures, including those which inhabit these islands, and some of the Englishes beyond them.

This may be true even though readers whose imaginative world has been largely constructed by translated works – the readers of *MPT* for example – would endorse without a second's hesitation the positives of translation, facing down the doubt that cripplingly stresses the imaginative or cultural or linguistic distance between original and translation. Not so much the 'possibility' of total translation, then, but the total impossibility of not having translations. How could one's mind have done without – in my case – the Bible in the Authorised Version of 1611, Lattimore's Homer, Cohen's Cervantes, Constance Garnett's Turgenev, David Magarshark's Dostoevsky, Waley's Chinese poems, and so on? Or without

The Penguin Modern European Poets series? Or without Jerome Rothenberg's *Technicians of the Sacred*, Ruth Finnegan's *Oral Poetry*, Judith Gleeson's *Leaf and Bone*?

But in the world of the poem that lies beyond the confines of dedicated magazines, there is perhaps a need for renewed commitment to the foreign-language poem-in-translation, and the poem in English that, because it belongs to earlier times or a non-English English, needs a different kind of 'translation', an interpretative, creative reading without formal translation. One argument which could be made more often 'in favour' of translation (George Steiner makes it, in the Introduction referred to above) is to suggest that in the normal activity of reading our own literature, we continuously 'translate'. Reading the English of then, from say the fourteenth to the twentieth centuries, into the English of now inside our heads, it's obvious that there are words, rhythms, stresses, that we have to translate:

> I that in heill wes, and gladnes,
> Am trublit now wiyth gret seiknes,
> And feblit with infermite.
> Timor mortis conturbat me.
> **William Dunbar, late 15th-16th century.**

I'm not sure if the 'e' of 'feblit' is long or short – short I guess. Are 'gladnes' and 'seiknes' two long syllables each or a short and a long? I find it a tremendous verse without being sure of my 'translation' as I read. Then I 'hear' the stressed 'me' at the end and the second reading persuades the ear that 'gladnes' and 'seikness' are two long syllables, and that the 'ei' of 'heill' and 'seik' is heard as a diphthong. And in this act of reading-translating what seems crucial is that the sound and texture of the original, the English of then, is not overlaid by the English of now. One might think 'sickness' but hear, or strive to hear, 'seikness'.

Chaucer is perhaps easier to read-translate, but hearing his unmistakable five-stress line involves de-remembering, or not letting rise to the surface of the auditory memory, other five-stress lines – Wallace Stevens', Shelley's, Browning's, Shakespeare's and so on. It's hardly straining the term to suggest that the act of hearing these lines involves a kind of 'translation' – and of course not just of nouns like 'pye' and 'jargon'.

> He was al coltissh, full of ragerye,
> And ful of jargon as a flekked pye.
> The slakke skin aboute his nekke shaketh,
> While that he sang, so chaunteth he and craketh.
>
> **Chaucer**, *Merchant's Tale*.

The same consideration works in geographical or cultural terms. The readers of various Englishes need to subjugate themselves to and imaginatively create, starting from their own English, the tunes, the rhythms and syntactic habits of other Englishes as they read. Because William Carlos Williams' English isn't Derek Walcott's and neither is Les Murray's.

This kind of interpretative reading, this imaginative quasi-translation, can only take place in the absence of full translation in the formal sense – a different printed version, 'simplifying' things. Formal translation offered when none is needed becomes an attempt to supplant – the dialect with the standard for instance, the authentic with the smoothed out. We have become familiar with this lethal form of supplantive translation in the editorial erosions of Emily Dickinson. Fine poet though he was, Richard Wilbur published, as late as 1960, an edition (Signet) of her selected poems which reproduces earlier interferences with her texts, even though the authentic or original versions were by then available. Side by side are the original first line of Poem 258 in Johnson's 1951 Faber edition and Wilbur's.

There's a certain Slant of light,	There's a certain slant of light,
Winter Afternoons –	On winter afternoons,
That oppresses, like the Heft	That oppresses, like the weight
Of Cathedral Tunes –	Of cathedral tunes.

The process of smoothing down Emily Dickinson produced remarkable alterations of meaning. In Poem 303, 'The Soul selects her own Society – / Then – shuts the Door –', those first lines are without dashes in Wilbur, then he alters the 'To' of line 3 to 'On' and introduces an 'Obtrude' in line 4 to replace 'Present', making an imperative clause out of an adjective phrase.

| To her divine Majority – | On her divine majority |
| Present no more – | Obtrude no more. |

In the second verse the Wilbur edition recasts the participle 'pausing' as a glib gerund, and in line 3 makes the emperor 'unmoved', not the Soul.

Unmoved – she notes the Chariots –	Unmoved, she notes the chariot's
pausing –	pausing
At her low Gate –	At her low gate;
Unmoved – an Emperor be kneeling –	Unmoved, an emperor is kneeling
Upon her Mat –	Upon her mat.

Instead of assuming that the reader has the skill to perform any necessary reworking – interpretative translating – of difficult verses in his or her head, the editor nervously replaces the true music of the poem with an alternative simpler version, a musak, one might say, feeling a need to translate formally as if from another language, when the only 'translation' that's needed takes place in the head. Why not then edit-translate *Huckleberry Finn*, for instance?

Doubt about the young or mature reader's capacity inferentially to construct from what he or she already knows the whole of the partly audible, partly known poem becomes a denial of both reader's and writer's skills. One reason for the relative neglect of dialect poetry (not least in anthologies for schools) may be the spurious idea that it needs replacing – in formal printed translation – so as to be understood by non-dialect speakers, who just can't hear it right. My own dialect was broad Lancashire, but I 'hear' William Barnes with enormous pleasure, hear indeed one of the greatest lyricists:

'Ithin the woodlands, flowr'y gleaded,
   By the woak tree's mossy moot,
The sheenen grass-bleades, timber-sheaded,
   Now do quiver under voot;
An' birds do whissle over head,
An' water's bubblen in its bed,
An' there for me the apple tree
Do lean down low in Linden Lea.

Simplifying and smoothing down (and out), creating replacements, are respectable cultural activities. Chaucer done into rap for schoolchildren, or a BBC Shakespeare to be mainly prose with some patches of verse in it, and other such phenomena, as long as they are ends-in-themselves intended to permanently by-pass the original, deny translation in denying the plurality and provisionality of it, effacing both the original and the invitation to go back to it.

These thoughts about the indispensability to writer and reader of immersion in the processes of producing literal and literary translations, and in so doing going back to originals where possible, were prompted by a recent attempt to 'sell' Seferis and Ritsos to members of a writers' group. I provided the group with a transliteration, a word-for-word 'literal' translation, and two drafts of my own literary attempt, and above them the original Greek text of this short poem by Ritsos, one of '15 short songs for the bitter motherland'.

ΛΑΟΣ – Populace

Μικροσ λαοσ και πολεμα διχωσ σπαθια και βολια
για ολου του κοσμου το ψωμι, το φωσ και το
τραγουδι.

Κατω απ τι γλωσσα του κρατει τουσ βογγουσ και τα
ζητω
κι αν κανει πωσ τα τραγουδει ραγιζουν τα λιθαρια.

Μικροσ λαοσ και πολεμα διχωσ σπαθια και βολια
meecros laos kay polema theekos spathia kai volia
small people and it-fights without swords and bullets

για ολου του κοσμου το ψωμι, το φωσ και το
τραγουδι.
yia olloo too kosmoo to psomi to fos keh to tragouthee
for all of-the of-world the bread the light and the song

Κατω απ τι γλωσσα του κρατει τουσ βογγουσ και τα
ζητω
catto ap tee glossa too kratei toos vongous key ta zeeto
underneath the tongue of-it it-holds the howls and the
    hurrahs

κι αν κανει πωσ τα τραγουδει ραγιζουν τα λιθαρια.
ke an kanei pos ta tragouthi ragizoon ta litharia
and if it-makes that them it-sings crack the boulders.

draft 1

A small populace / people – it fights/ and they fight without
    swords or bullets
For the bread of all the world, for its light, its song.

Beneath the tongue it holds the howls and hurrahs
And if it decides / should it be moved to sing them –
    boulders break apart/ will crack open.

draft 2

A small people, fighting without swords or bullets
for the all the world's bread, and light, and song.

Under its tongue it keeps screams and rejoicing
and once it decides to sing them, rocks will split open..

The translated outcome was less the point for me than the
illuminating group process of moving between the original
text with crudish transliteration, and the literal rendering and
draft translation. Clearly, if only **draft 2** had been available to
those new – apart from one – readers of Ritsos, the power of
that short poem might not have been as deeply felt and
appreciated. Add in the consideration that the sequence as a
whole, which is not the most self-evidently lyrical, was set to
music by Theodorakis and become part of a popular sung
tradition, and one's sense of the accessibility of the poem-
in-translation, and its worth or value, are challenged by a
newly discovered strangeness.

Csokits remarks that Ted Hughes had the knack of seeing,
as in X-ray, through the literal version he was provided with to
the bone-structure of the original Pilinsky. Most of us may
have less of that seeing gift, and find another metaphor more
appropriate. For instance the Maya myth that describes how
the gods jealously punished newly created humankind for the
presumption of its all-seeing intelligence:

And the Creator and Maker took flints of obsidian
and chipped at the clear surface of their creatures' gaze,
and blew mist into their eyes and clouded them over
so they saw the world as if in a misted-up mirror.

So at the beginning of time, the first clear wisdom
of men and women was taken from them,
and their understanding was dimmed for ever.

This 'imitation' of a translation of a translation might seem
a pessimistic metaphor for the encounter with the translated
poem; it might be thought quite bracing, though, as well.

Reviews

Tristan Corbière
Wry-Blue Loves: Les Amours Jaunes *and Other Poems*
Translated and introduced by Peter Dale
Anvil Press Poetry Ltd
London 2005
ISBN 0-85646-377-9
478pp. paperback £14.95 $24.95 in USA

A detail in Peter Dale's introduction stands out: in 1869, Tristan Corbière returned from Italy to his native Morlaix, where 'he outraged the locals by appearing on the balcony in a bishop's vestments which he had brought from Rome'. The Catholic church was a powerful authority in Second Empire France, and therefore an ideal target for this poet. His 'Serenade of Serenades', for example, is a string of resolutely carnal and blasphemous intercessions addressed to a 'Virgin' more diabolical dominatrix than mild saviouress.

The over-arching title of the work gives us the 'colour' of the poetry. Peter Dale has translated 'Les Amours Jaunes' as 'Wry-blue loves'. 'Blue' contributes – anachronistically but effectively – smutty, kinky, melancholy, uneasy, boozy, while suggesting the outsider status and orality of the Blues. In the French, yellow is the colour of the cuckold, the traitor, the pariah, and the outcast Jew. It suggests staining, pollution, illness, death and the 'rire jaune' of one for whom life is a tragic joke.

The title also embodies the spirit of contradiction that runs through the work: 'Amours' attracts, 'Jaunes' repels, negatives correct or cancel positives. These shifting loyalties give his verse its feeling of instability, like the rolling and pitching of a ship. But the 'loves', although signified with an off-hand plural, do exist: love of women, Brittany, life, the sea. Loves that lead to exuberance, recklessness, rule-breaking.

The more repressive the authority, the more powerful and meaningful – and for a non-conformist, enjoyable – the act of breaking a law becomes. Corbière lines up rules like toy soldiers, then cannons them. 'I Sonnet' is an attack on the Parnassian School (the self-appointed 'poetry police' of the time). Corbière subverts the strict sonnet in alexandrines, denouncing it, in their hands, as little more than a set of instructions for use, a blueprint, or 'sacred telegram' – a barrier (although clearly ineffectual here) to upsurges of dangerous, fire-brand creativity.

The poet's ironic use of pastiche, cliché and quotation (Musset, Lamartine, Baudelaire, Ronsard, Villon), his disjunctive punctuation, his recognisable subversion of fixed or traditional forms (sonnet, rondeau, ballad, laisse), all show how attached he is to his heritage, even as he rejects it. Contemporary France was marked by a similar tug-of-war, and it is tempting to see the reflection of this in his work. After all, the thirty years of Corbière's life (1845-1875) included the June Days, Louis-Napoléon's *coup-d'état*, the Siege of Paris, and the Commune.

Peter Dale, in translating Corbière, faced some of the more robust barriers that may stand between languages: deciphering puns, allusions and obsolete slang, or rendering the idiosyncrasy of Corbière's versification in a different poetic tradition. His aim is 'to find equivalents to the form of Corbière's poems' and the result is to be judged as 'the work of a poet rather than a scholar'. Here is an example of what he achieves within the conditions he sets himself:

> Renegade, this one. Defaulter, wandering:
>   Does anything not to do a thing.
> Drifts nowhere and beyond; swashbuckler, yob,
> Privateer, two-faced, on shipboard or shore job;
> Lackey, freebooter, black, white, soldier – hired –
> Hit-man, does anything and all required, [. . .]

('Renegade', *Seafarers*)

He is good at striking a particular tone of voice, as this shifts between sections, and from poem to poem:

> Sands of old bones – And the tide coughs
> Up death-knells, kicking buckets of noisy spray . . .
> – Pallid salt marsh where the moon scoffs
> Fat worms to while the night away.

('Ill-Boding Landscape', *Armorica*)

His decision to give form the upper hand is justifiable in so far as Corbière often initiates meaning through word-play. However, because rhymes are easier to find in French than in English, and are therefore often less significant, this decision constantly pulls him towards a denser texture. Although he finds ways to compensate – such as increasing enjambment to lighten end-rhyme – in many passages, sense is pushed into second place by the need for ingenuity, while imagery and word order are warped by appendages:

– Je la trouvai – bien des printemps,
Bien des vingt ans, bien des vingt francs,
Bien des trous et bien de la lune
Après – Toujours vierge et vingt ans,
Et . . . colonelle à la Commune!

– I found her – many springs, post me,
Many score years, score francs in fee,
Many holes burnt, much moonings blank
After – Still virgin and twenty . . . rank:
Colonel to the Commune – to be frank!

'À la mémoire de Zulma VIERGE-FOLLE HORS BARRIÈRE
et d'un louis', (*Les Amours Jaunes*)

However, the present discussion highlights the challenges of
the task in hand; it does not diminish the courage, generosity
and verve of Peter Dale's undertaking. This bilingual, compre-
hensive edition, complete with introduction and endnotes,
achieves what it sets out to do: provide English readers with 'a
fair impression of Corbière's method and essence'.

Olivia McCannon

Horace
The Odes: New verse translation with facing Latin text
and notes
translated by Colin Sydenham
G. Duckworth & Co
ISBN 0 7516 3431 3
pb 287pp, £16.99.

'Horace has been translated more often into more languages
than any other author, [outside] . . . the Bible,' says the
foreword to this book. 'Generations of schoolboys' can be added
to the tally.

Horace's personality is better-known than most of his
writings. Colin Sydenham has come to share that personality:
convivial, reflective, humorous. The Horatian Society, his
brainchild, dines annually in force. His book is a work of deep
and lifelong love. He was fortunate to study under D.P.
Simpson and others at Eton, and L.P. Wilkinson at King's,
Cambridge. He says he is neither scholar nor poet. Housman
said at Trinity: 'Gentlemen! This college has seen Wordsworth
drunk and Porson sober. I stand before you, a better scholar
than Wordsworth, a better poet than Porson.' Sydenham could
say the same. His scholarship is impeccable, never too heavy. In
his text there is fine poetry and exceptional craftsmanship.
Here is Europa: 'One moment she was in the fields, intent/ on
plaiting for the Nymphs a promised wreath,/ next all she dimly
saw was stars above/ and waves beneath.' Almost all his Odes
rhyme, in moderation, and all scan, thus matching but not
mimicking Horace's discipline. His rhymes are, as he puts it,
genuine. His line-lengths reflect those of Horace, in their great
variety. Nearly all his text is iambic, or trochaic; dactylic lines
come in just where they are well-suited. A translator into verse
may as well use familiar English metres: the task is already
difficult enough.

Sydenham's book is 'principally designed for the inexpert'
reader. His object is 'to produce a version which can be read

with pleasure'. He has succeeded. Likewise his exemplary
Notes are not for the few real experts. Others, though, will
cherish this book, especially if they have some Latin. And for
newcomers to Horace, here is the way in.

Horace's great feat was to adapt Greek lyric metres to the
more ponderous Latin tongue, writing beautiful poetry. And to
do well in difficult times! Sydenham argues that a translation
into free verse would not convey what is fundamental to
Horace's lyrics, his metrical discipline. We would not discard,
say, Ted Hughes' free verse Ovid or E.V. Rieu's prose Homer
on such grounds. Ovid and Homer were equally unprecedented
technical masters, and also have great narratives to sweep us
along. But Sydenham uses rhyme and metre extremely well.

As we know from the rules of copyright, any poem, however
short, is a complete work. It follows that the philosophy of the
Odes need not be consistent. The speed of Horace's thought,
the many confusions and allusions, are unobtrusively clarified
in the text or notes. Sydenham tells how the moralising first
stanza of 'Integer vitae' (I. 22) has been sung at funerals, even
though Horace soon subverts the high tone. The good man
needs no darts and poisoned arrows: he has heaven's protection,
worldwide: he can go about unarmed and carefree. A wolf fled
from Horace – his sweetheart Lalage was there. Extremes of
climate can be ignored – with Lalage. She will shield him, says
Sydenham, adding the word 'shield' to make it clear. To what
has sometimes appeared incomprehensible, he brings insight
and vigour. We may see Horace as not mocking but upholding
virtue; he is also good company for the reader. He smiles about
dropping his shield at Philippi, but only because he fought on
the wrong side. He and Lalage were free agents: he was himself
'integer vitae scelerisque purus'.

Sydenham matches diction to context. Here, the stately: 'Of
lovely mother daughter lovelier still . . .' Elsewhere, 'the verbal
avuncular cosh'. A pleasing passage is III. 22: quam . . . / verris
obliquum meditantis ictum / sanguine donem: 'I'll gladly
sacrifice / . . . a young boar, practising / his sidelong slice.'

All the Odes come into focus. Book Three travels from the
six severe Alcaic odes, the extreme honour of long-dead
Regulus, to the merriment of the wine-jar. Book Four, which
looks so obsequious, now reveals its merits. Housman's
favourite is recognised, corruptible Lollius is immortalised,
Caesar idolised:

'longas o utinam, dux bone, ferias
praestes Hesperiae!' dicimus integro
sicci mane die, dicimus uvidi,
ut sol Oceano subest. (IV.5)

'Long be the carefree time that Caesar grants
to Italy.' This prayer is on our lips
   (dry in the morning, moistened later, as
   the sun in Ocean dips).

Horace mixes his themes: late love strikes hard; the poet's no
Pindar; Lyce looks old. Drusus wins battles, Virgil, a jar!
(IV.12) 'Now's the time to season/ prudence with folly; it's a
joy to take/ a holiday from reason': dulce est desipere in loco.

This volume is a delight, beautifully written and presented.
For light relief, the multiple versions of Franklin P. Adams can
be found on the Web.

Timothy Adès

Richard Burns
Black Light: Poems in memory of George Seferis
King of Hearts, Norwich (3rd edition) 1995
ISBN 0 9518657
pb 28pp, £4.95

Richard Burns
Mavro Fos: Poiimata eis mnimin Yiorgou Seferi
translated by Nasos Vayenas, Ilias Layios
Lalon Ydor series no. 3, Typothito, Athens 2005
ISBN 960-402-186-9
pb 68pp, €6.73

'He was struck, as everyone is, by the light. Instead of being half absorbed into the object, as in England, in Greece the object seemed to give off light, as if lit from within.'
                              Roger Berthoud, *The Life of Henry Moore.*

There is good reason to describe Richard Burns as a European poet writing in English: equally interested in politico-historical issues and inner spaces, at ease with both established and experimental forms in short lyrics as well as long poems, his is a shape-shifting, encompassing voice, nourished by long spells in places like France, Greece, and former Yugoslavia. Burns draws from diverse influences, and finds common ground in Mediterranean, Balkan and Jewish traditions, attempting to align constants of humanity, to commune with affirmations of life, listen to the legacies of the dead. The poet who founded the Cambridge Poetry Festival three decades ago is now at the peak of his powers: *The Manager*, a 100-part, verse-paragraph cross-section of modern consciousness appeared in 2001, accompanied by the resounding praise that announces the truly significant. Another major work first conceived in the mid-eighties, *The Blue Butterfly*, inspired by a massacre of Serbs by the Nazis at Kragujevac in 1941, has recently been published in its complete form.

An earlier highpoint in Burns's output grew from his relationship with Greece, and his sensed bonds with one of its Nobel laureates, George Seferis. The seeds of *Black Light* can be traced to observations Seferis records in his journal in June 1946 (there we read that '. . . behind the grey and golden weft of the Attic summer exists a *frightful black* . . . we are all of us the playthings of this black'); shortly after, they infiltrate his long poem 'The Thrush'. In twelve poems exploring the meeting of cultures and staging amalgamations of languages and literary voices, Burns pursues this intimation of death/black, which forever follows, and enables light/life, as it chimes with his own experience of the Greek landscape and people. So we find the Greek poet in Burns, Burns in (Seferis's) Greece:

> So no charts, friend, this exacting light defeats them, just as the
>   waves cancel our wake:
> we're on our way to an island, and all I know is, I'm helplessly
>   in love with this mountain and this sea,
> for here desire and fulfilment are stitched in one weft of light,
>   cross-woven, stilled and impossible to unravel
> from this seamless tide of days which flow in one movement together,
>   its whole fabric soaked and doubly strengthened in salt,
> and mine is its crusted harvest with the perfect inner sheen,
>   although I have gnawed summer down to its black core.
>   ('Salt')

It all unfolds with a sense of resolve and clarity of vision often reminiscent of Eliot's *Four Quartets,* and in an array of forms – from the villanelles 'In Memory of George Seferis' which open and close the sequence, to the prose poetry of 'Shell' – that witness the measured immediacy of Burns's diction synchronizing with the metaphysical substrata lurking in the apparent warmth of his chosen surroundings: a taverna, waterfronts in sunset, Pelion, the constant drone of cicadas 'like waves of an inland sea'. Being there, Burns strives to decipher a pre-verbal, primary experience that has already called for insistent retellings. In this he is assisted by Seferis, whose spectre arrives in 'Neolithic' to remind him that 'light is mirrored in blood . . . dark and light are one', and whose vision Burns's originals are also among the best translations of, a prime example of poetry understood by poetry.

While further enunciating presences of translation and dialogue in the poetic act, *Black Light*'s intertextual intricacies (translations of the related passages from Seferis's journal and 'The Thrush' open the collection; lines of his become epigraphs to all, and are found embedded or transmuted within most, poems; Burns's 'notes and acknowledgements' disclose an affluence of literary and cultural absorptions) serve to accent the workings of empathy, they intimate manifold cognitions and desires between living and writing. As Burns's dialogue with both his 'Greek experience' and the universals of transience progresses, these poems emerge as not just 'in memory' but equally *of memory*; for *Black Light* is above all a sustained meditation on its callings, and on imperatives of survival within the creative condition: if 'black is the light behind the blaze of day/ and dark the core beneath its coloured coat', as 'In Memory of George Seferis (II)' tells us, then you must 'devour it, lest it eat your soul away'.

Both textual vertigo and a sense of true homecoming arrive with a new, bilingual edition in which these poems, already so drenched in what is Greek, are faced with their Greek translations. In part because translation, here, will also coincide with un-translation: the fragments of Seferis in English revert to the originals, italicised transliterations of words like *koré* or *tsípouro* and other cultural appropriations disappear into a 'target language' now claiming its own fabric. Responsible for echoing the encounter of Burns and Seferis are two poets, Nasos Vayenas* and Ilias Layios, each rendering half of *Black*

---

*It is worth noting that Vayenas has long been conversing with Burns: the latter translated Vayenas's second collection, *Biography* in 1978 (seeds of Burns' own *The Messenger* can be detected here); in turn, Vayenas included a translation of 'Only the Common Miracle' from *Black Light*, in a collection he published in 1989; the acknowledgements of *Black Light* refer to Vayenas's 1979 study of Seferis, *The Poet and the Dancer*, as one of the many influences behind the sequence.

Light's poems. It is inevitable that their respective poetic accents be sensed; as is their consensus that translation must unravel original and itself in order to really take place. Insight into the nature of what is undertaken, together with considerable verbal agility, brings mesmerizing renderings that are themselves nothing short of poetry in Greek; a sureness of touch exudes from every line.

Mavro Fos emerges as a game of mirrors where originals conspire with translations toward scenes of recognition: the translating that attends the poetry is allowed to surface, translations reveal what they share with literary creation, the two poet-translators glimpse their own reflection in what Burns has made. We confront a quartet of sensibilities in multi-layered, many-sided conversation that lays bare interdependences of poetry, translation, and influence. There is an overwhelming sense not only of the constitution and essences of Burns's originals being most aptly reverberated across these arenas of dialogue, but of a further completion effected, a new whole that sees Seferis's 'black light' more illuminated than ever. It is then apposite that *Mavro Fos* closes with a newly added prose piece by Burns ('An Old Man at the Harbour') that directly imagines an encounter with the Greek poet. It makes for a poignant coda to this polyphonic book, one that is also – as often happens with poetry publications in Greece – a work of art in itself.

Paschalis Nikolaou

Piotr Sommer
Continued
translated by Halina Janod et al,
Bloodaxe Books
ISBN 1-85224-702-9
pb 128pp £8.95

Arjen Duinker, W N Herbert, Uwe Kolbe,
Peter Laugesen, Karine Martel and Yang Lian
Sailor's Home: A Miscellany of Poetry
Shearsman Books
ISBN 0-907562-86-8
pb 132pp £9.95

Continued is an expanded version of the leading Polish poet, Piotr Sommer's, earlier *Things to Translate*, containing about fifty translations from his various collections, by Halina Janod with John Ashbery, Douglas Dunn, D.J. Enright and others. By starting with the more recent poems, it allows us to taste the best wine first, though even his earlier – often more narrative – poems, contain the seeds of his mature voice with its quirky take on life's banality. Sommer focuses on continuity through history, language and objects, but argues that it cannot be accurately recorded, as the weighted lines of 'Tomorrow' suggests: 'Whoever lives on will tell us how it was; whoever survives/ the rest will tell it more precisely'. Occasional affirmation, such as in 'Morning on Earth' ('nothing's/ at odds with anything'), is frequently undermined by low-key, self-deprecation as in 'Visibility': 'I haven't figured out who/ I'm saying this to, or even who/ would care . . .' Repeatedly we see tedium and novelty travel hand in hand in an oddly satisfying way.

Consider 'Believe me' where he elevates an everyday frustration to something of metaphysical import:

You're not going to find a better place
for these cosmetics, even if eventually
we wind up with some sort of bathroom cabinet and
you stop knocking them over with your towel—
there'll still be a thousand reasons to complain
and a thousand pieces of glass on the floor
and a thousand new worries
and we'll still have to get up early.

In 'Don't sleep, take notes' this quotidian life is presented with dark humour, and ominous overtones of Poland before communist collapse:

If I don't produce the receipt,
if I don't find the receipt,
the milk woman will cut our throats.

Sommer repeatedly provides an understated, quietly assertive argument. Though there is certainly bleakness – our lives can be mislaid like objects, or nature itself is 'under warranty' – we are all part of a continuum, albeit one we can't get too excited about. In 'Continued' he states: 'Nothing will be the same as it was/ and that too will be new somehow', here, like Shakespeare, using simple diction for subtle expression. We see this again below in the seamless way his raises the level of the ordinary:

All memory we owe to objects
which adopt us for life and
tame us with touch, smell
and rustle. That's why it's so hard
for them to part with us: they guide us
till the end . . .

                  ('A certain tree in Powazki Cemetery')

Piotr Sommer's poetry needs to be treated with respect. It gives you something new each time you go back to it.

Seeing the old Sailor's Home building in Ghent, suggested to the Chinese poet Yang Lian a connection between the sailor and the poet's life, as the book's blurb puts it: 'many years of travel, cross-cultural contacts, a place of rest after too much time on the high seas'. The result is *Sailor's Home*, a multilingual collaboration between himself and five 'poet-friends', each left free to explore individual interpretations of the idea. The poems are also provided in their original languages.

Arjen Duinker (Dutch) and Karine Martel (French) both use the sea as a metaphor for language. Duinker interweaves sexual and linguistic sensuality: 'Extremities of words in clouds of thick smoke . . ./ The ship disguises the ways through the idiom'. The ocean is a vast arena for creativity: 'The heart of the ocean keeps on expanding . . .' His poems are sometimes too driven by lists but he also has some hauntingly ambiguous lines: 'Where the flower shows her beauty/ Butterflies take salt from the sea.' Karine Martel is a poet for those who love the avant-garde. Her sequence stems from a real setting and then moves into more abstract meditations on aridity and plenitude. Though the incantatory effect of some of her lines is lost in translation, at its best the poetry is very uplifting, with moving descriptions of the word's evolution out of chaos, such as this description of 'the sea's surge':

It knows only the speech of silence.
It has left eternity behind it.
It knows only transparency.
The swell was born on the wave of the world.

Described by the Guardian as 'a weird mix of Desperate Dan, MacDiarmid and Dostoyevsky', W N Herbert (Scottish) brings the subject matter firmly back to earth with poems rich in concrete detail related to seafaring: ships, lighthouses, fishing tackle, the harshness of the elements as well as a lost industry. The language is unashamedly alliterative, frequently onomatopoeic with sinuous, consonantal layering. Take this wonderful ship image: 'its high-hipped arse of galleon', or this vividly accurate picture of a lighthouse:

> In Winter the Old High Light speaks
> the language of the sea winds
> and the hail: cold unwraps itself, sheet
> after sheet, around its weeping edge.

> In the spring it rediscovers sunlight,
> lets the clouds peel off like gulls
> from its lead-lidded eyeball. The earth wind mouths
> against the landing door, yammering and keen.

For those new to Herbert's poetry, this selection will have you completely hooked.

Uwe Kolbe (German) and Peter Laugesen (Danish), both writing with dry humour in a conversational style, focus on the sailor himself. For Kolbe, the nomadic sailor is the perfect metaphor for failed relationships. He turns the notion of the sailor with a woman in every port on its head, well translated by Jo Tudor: 'I don't do waiting'. Particularly effective is the way he manages to pack emotion into such simple statements, as in 'Sailor's All': '

> But what stays
> is a love poem,
> a little insistent song—
> almost nothing.

The sailor of Peter Laugesen's poems is also endearing. There is humour, poignancy and indeed something profound being said about the human condition here. Take the Willy Loman-like character in 'Sailor', 'a little guy/ who did his best'; for although inadequate ' It is his sea/ he will sail out there'. He wraps up the portrayal with humorous wordplay in 'The Sailor's Blues':

I am a
loose cannon
on a sinking ship

Yang Lian concludes with rich, sensuous, life-affirming poems superbly translated by Brian Holtom. Like Walt Whitman, he merges the natural and sexual into a cosmic/ pantheistic whole: 'father's swollen dropped scrotum hangs down/ like a constellation wriggling children's undeniable destiny'. Note Holtom's subtle rhyming and sound patterns in 'Shore':

filled with the sexiness of a final stare   candle-flame's
    x-ray visage
shore a transparent structure in the flesh of lovemaking
we are each other's anchor   we are each other's anchorage

Thus, a chance observation by Yang Lian has given birth to a wealth of fine poems which, though commissioned, do not read as such.

Belinda Cooke

Shorter Reviews & Further Books Received

New from Anvil:

Jacques Réda, *Treading Lightly: Selected Poems 1961-1975*, translated by Jennie Feldman, 141pp, paperback, £8.95, ISBN 0-85646-380-9
   Impressive translations of this important French poet.

New from Arc Visible Poets:

Sabine Lange, *The Fishermen Sleep*, translated by Jenny Williams/introduced by Mary O'Donnell, 116pp, paperback, £8.95, ISBN 1-904614-20-5
   Williams captures German poet Sabine Lange's deceptively simple lyrics with great skill and sensitivity.

Inna Lisnianskaya, *Far From Sodom*, translated by Daniel Weissbort/introduced by Elaine Feinstein, 105pp, paperback, £8.95, ISBN 1-904614-14-0
   With Weissbort's masterly translations and Feinstein's knowledgeable introduction to the Russian poet, an exemplary template for a translation volume.

Cathal Ó Searcaigh, *By the Hearth in Mín a'Leá*, translated by Frank Sewell, Denise Blake and Seamus Heaney, 174pp, paperback, £10.95, ISBN 1-904614-21-3
   A well-deserved Poetry Book Society Recommendation, this volume brings Ó Searcaigh's personal and often intense poems to English readers for the first time, extremely well-served by a trio of illustrious translators.

Georg Trakl, *To the Silenced*, translated and introduced by Will Stone, 165pp, paperback, £10.95, ISBN 1-904614-10-8

Stone's excellent edition of the unduly neglected Austrian poet is sure to revive interest in Trakl's work; sensitive translations with admirably detailed introductory essay and biographical information.

New Books from Black Widow Press

Tristan Tzara, *Chanson Dada: Selected Poems*, translated and introduced by Lee Harwood, 144pp, paperback, $17.95, ISBN 0-9768449-0-7

Tristan Tzara, *Approximate Man and other writings*, translated and introduced by Mary Ann Caws, 290pp, paperback, $19.95, ISBN 0-9768449-1-5

Two inaugural volumes from America's new Black Widow Press focusing on the legendary Dada poet.

New Books from Cló Iar-Chonnachta

Gabriel Rosenstock, *Selected Poems*, translated by Paddy Bushe, 193pp, paperback, €14, ISBN 1-902420-95-0

Louis de Paor, *Clapping in the Cemetery*, translated by the author with Biddy Jenkinson, Mary O'Donoghue and Kevin Anderson, 232 pp, paperback, €14, ISBN 1-902420-94-2

Two volumes from the Connemara publishers bringing renowned Irish poets to a new English audience.

New Books from Shearsman

Ilma Rakusa, *A Farewell to Everything: ninety nine-liners* translated by Andrew Shields and Andrew Winnard, 101 pp, paperback, £9.95, ISBN 0-907562-77-9

A wonderful edition of Slovakian poet's Rakusa's 1997 German collection, *Ein Strich durch alles*, providing what it says on the can, ninety exquisite nine-line poems, deftly translated by Shields and Winnard.

César Vallejo, *Trilce,* translated and introduced by Michael Smith and Valentino Gianuzzi, 256pp, paperback, £12.95, ISBN 0-907562-72-8

César Vallejo, *Complete Later Poems,* translated and introduced by Michael Smith and Valentino Gianuzzi, 420pp, paperback, £16.95, ISBN 0-907562-73-6

Two major new volumes exploring the work of the great Peruvian poet. Highly recommended.

New Books from Southword Editions

Andres Ehin, *Moose Beetle Swallow*, translated from the Estonian by Patrick Cotter, 64pp, paperback, £8, ISBN 1-905002-13-0

Guntars Godins, *Flying Blind*, translated from the Latvian by Eugene O'Connell, 61pp, paperback, £8, ISBN 1-905002-12-2

Lázló Lator, *The Belling*, translated from the Hungarian by Gregory O'Donoghue, Liz O'Donoghue, Eugene O'Connell and Patrick Cotter with the help of Zsuzsa Kiss, 62pp, paperback, £8, ISBN 1-905002-14-9

Three more excellent volumes, bringing an admirable new selection of Eastern European poetry into English.

Also Received:

Mary Värme, *The Lord of Misrule: a poem in five acts.* English version by Glenn Storhaug, 59pp, hardback, Éditions Poisson & d'Étioles, ISBN, 91-631-6782-4

Mary Värme, *Vanstyrets herre: Dikt i fem akter*, 59pp, hardback, Éditions Poisson & d'Étioles, ISBN, 91-631-3653-81

A ground-breaking dual publication of Norwegian poet Värme's 2003 work, in two separate but twinned editions, one offering the original, one Storhaug's new version, both beautifully produced.

Books for review should be sent to Josephine Balmer, Reviews Editor, *Modern Poetry in Translation,* East Meon, St John's Road, Crowborough, East Sussex, TN6 1RW.

(Please note that in the next issue we will be offering a round-up of far-eastern poetry.)

Acknowledgements

The Editors are grateful to the following publishers for permissions:

Gallimard, to publish Olivia McCannon's translations of Jean Follain's 'Frustes repas', 'Le buveur de bière', 'La mangeuse d'amandes', 'L'avant-conception' (from *Usage du temps*); 'Glace rouge', 'L'oeuf' and 'Le retour' (from *Territoires*). Copyright Editions Gallimard, Paris.

S. Fischer Verlag, to publish Ruth Ingram's translation of Hilde Domin's poem 'Wen es trifft', from *Gesammelte Gedichte*. Copyright S. Fischer Verlag, 1987.

Anvil Press, to publish Ruth Christie's translation of Nâzim Hikmet's poem 'On Living', from *Beyond the Walls*, 2002. Copyright Mehmet Hikmet and Ruth Christie.

Notes on Contributors

Timothy Adès wrote Latin and Greek verse at school, read Classics at university and studied international business management. He has won various awards as a translator-poet working mostly with rhyme and metre.

Charles Cantalupo is the author of the book of poems, *Light the Lights* (Red Sea Press, 2004), and three books of translations of Eritrean poetry. He has written and directed the new documentary, *Against All Odds: African Languages and Literatures into the 21st Century*. He is professor at Penn State University.

Belinda Cooke's poetry, reviews and Russian translations have been published widely. She is currently completing an edition of *The Selected Poems of Marina Tsvetaeva*. She lives in Aberdeenshire.

Quentin S Crisp studied Japanese at Durham University and has researched Japanese literature at Kyoto University. He has had three volumes of short stories published, *The Nightmare Exhibition* (BJM Press 2001), *Morbid Tales* (Tartarus Press 2004), and *Rule Dementia!* (Rainfall Books 2005).

Sasha Dugdale is a consultant and translator for the Royal Court Theatre. Her first collection *Notebook* was published by Carcanet/Oxford Poets in 2003; her second, *The Estate*, is due out in 2007. Her translations of Tatiana Shcherbina, *Life Without: Selected Poetry and Prose*, were published by Bloodaxe in 2004.

Ruth Fainlight has published thirteen collections of poems in England and the USA, as well as two volumes of short stories. Books of her poems have appeared in Portuguese, French, Spanish and Italian translation. She received the Hawthornden and Cholmondeley Awards in 1998, and *Sugar-Paper Blue* (1997) was shortlisted for the 1998 Whitbread Award. Her new collection, *Moon Wheels,* is out this year, 2006.

Dorothea Grünzweig, born in Korntal, Germany in 1952, studied German and English at the Universities of Tübingen and Bangor. After a period of research on G.M. Hopkins at Oxford and a teaching position at the Scottish University of Dundee, she worked at a boarding school in southern Germany. Except for brief terms as writer-in-residence in Scotland and Germany, since 1989 she has lived in Helsinki, Finland, where she writes and translates works by Finnish and English-language poets. She has published three collections of poems, *Mittsommerschnitt* (1997), for which she received the Lyrikpreis der Stiftung Niedersachsen/ Wolfenbüttel (poetry prize from the state of Lower Saxony), *Vom Eisgebreit (From the Ice Field)* 2000, and *Glasstimmen lasinäänet (Glass Voice lasinäänet)* 2004, for which she received the Christian-Wagner Prize for Poetry – all with Wallstein Verlag, Göttingen.

Marilyn Hacker is the author of eleven collections of poetry, including *Desesperanto* (Norton, 2003). A *New and Selected Poems* is forthcoming from Carcanet/Oxford Poets in 2006. She is the translator of Vénus Khoury-Ghata's *She Says* (Graywolf, 2003) and Claire Malroux's *Birds and Bison* (Sheep Meadow, 2004), among other titles.

Michael Hamburger's *Collected Poems* were published in 1995. His *Poems of Paul Celan* came out in 1988 and the fourth edition of his *Friedrich Hölderlin, Poems and Fragments* in 2004.

Justin Hill was born in the Bahamas and grew up in North Yorkshire. He has written four books including *Passing Under Heaven* (winner of Somerset Maughan Award 2005 and short-listed for the 2005 Encore Award) which tells the story of Yu Xuanji's life; *Ciao Asmara* (shortlisted for the Thomas Cook Award 2003); and *The Drink and Dream Teahouse* (Betty Trask Award 2001 and 2001 Geoffrey Faber Memorial Prize).

Robert Hull has written many books for children, including two single-author verse collections, *Stargrazer,* from Hodder, and *Everest and Chips,* OUP. *Behind the Poem* is a full-length study of children writing poems. His second volume of poems from Peterloo Poets is due out in spring 2007.

Ruth Ingram, born Monika Ruth Heller 1927 in Berlin, the daughter of Hermann Heller (a Jewish Professor of International Law and Politics) and granddaughter of the poet Gustav Falke, came to England as a refugee in 1937. She was a lecturer and then Course Director for a postgraduate Course in Applied Social Studies. Since retiring she has worked with textiles and begun to write and to translate poetry.

W. D. Jackson was born in Liverpool in 1947. After studying English at Oxford, he went to live first in Italy and then, since 1973, in South Germany. His two books of poetry and translation, *Then and Now* (2002) and *From Now to Then* (2005) are published by Menard Press.

Ilmar Lehtpere's translations of Estonian poetry have appeared in a number of publications in the U.K., Ireland and the U.S. A volume of his translations of Doris Kareva's poetry will be published by Arc Publications.

John Lucas is Emeritus Professor of English at the universities of Loughborough and Nottingham Trent. He is the author of many critical books and of seven collections of poetry, most recently *The Long and the Short of It*. He is editor/publisher of Shoestring Press.

John Manson: retired teacher; was awarded the first Arts Council bursary for translation in Scotland in 1995. *Frae Glesca til Manila* (Markings, Kirkcudbright, 2000) collected some of his translations into Scots from French, Spanish, Italian and Portuguese. He has also translated poems by Aragon, Eluard and Neruda into English.

Olivia McCannon is currently working on a new version of Balzac's *Old Goriot* for Penguin Classics; she also translates contemporary French plays for the Royal Court. Her poems and stories have appeared in *Ambit*, the *Oxford Magazine*, *MPT* and the *Wolf*. She was awarded a Hawthornden Fellowship in 2005.

Hubert Moore's sixth full collection, *The Hearing Room*, is due this summer from Shoestring Press.

Paschalis Nikolaou has an Onassis Foundation scholarship at the University of East Anglia where he is completing a doctoral thesis on the interface of literary translation, creativity and autobiography. He is currently working on translations of the the poets Richard Burns and Nasos Vayenas.

J.P. Nosbaum's most recent publications include poems in *Poetry Review* and *Acumen* and reviews in *Poetry Wales*. Originally from the US, he has spent the last dozen years in Britain and currently lives in Cheltenham.

Bernard O'Donoghue teaches medieval English at Wadham College, Oxford. As well as five books of poems, he has published a parallel-text edition of medieval love poems, called *The Courtly Love Tradition* (Manchester University Press, 1982.)

Pascale Petit's latest collection *The Huntress* (Seren, 2005) was shortlisted for the TS Eliot Prize and was a *Times Literary Supplement* book of the year. A prizewinning pamphlet *The Wounded Deer − Fourteen poems after Frida Kahlo* (Smith Doorstop, 2005) was also published in 2005. In 2004 she was selected as a Next Generation Poet. She recently received an Arts Council of England award to take part in the 'Poet to Poet' translation project in China.

Susan Ranson: My father encouraged family poetry readings and an inspired teacher of German gave me some Rilke and said 'translate' − a task that has grown, alongside an interest in English punctuation and syntax as the sharpest of tools. Occasional published verse, and articles on language; in 2004 a study − apparently the first − on John Hopkins, the forceful and wayward sixteenth-century metrical psalmist.

Viara Tcholakova, a native of Bulgaria, has lived in the US since 1991. She collaborated with Roland Flint in translating Lyubomir Nikolov's poems in *Pagan*, Carnegie Mellon University Press, Pittsburgh, PA, 1992.

Derk Wynand, born in Bad Suderode, Germany in 1944, has lived in Canada since 1952. He has published 10 collections of poems, most recently, *Dead Man's Float,* Brick Books, 2002, a collection of fiction, and several books translated from the German of H.C. Artmann and Erich Wolfgang Skwara. His translation of Dorothea Grünzweig's first book appeared in a bilingual edition, *Midsummer Cut/ Mittsommerschnitt,* published by Buschek Books in 2002. He recently took early retirement from the University of Victoria's Dept. of Writing.

Alastair Thomson lived in Italy and Spain, before becoming Professor of English at universities in Britain, Africa, the Middle East, and Japan. He now lives in France, near Saint-Maixent.

Clive Wilmer is a Fellow of Sidney Sussex College, Cambridge. His wide range of published work includes seven volumes of his own poetry, the most recent of which are *Stigmata* (Worple, 2005) and *The Mystery of Things* (Carcanet, 2006). With George Gömöri he has translated five volumes of poetry from Hungarian, including *Forced March: Selected Poems* by Miklós Radnóti (Enitharmon, 2003).

Zhou Zan is a young poet and academic who has published individual poems widely in China. She is a specialist in modern Chinese poetry and has published books and essays on the subject. Poems of hers, translated by Pascale Petit, appeared in *MPT* 3/4.

MODERN POETRY IN TRANSLATION   Series 3   Number 1

INTRODUCTIONS

Edited by David and Helen Constantine
Cover by Chris Hyde

Contents

Price £11
Available from www.mptmagazine.com

MODERN POETRY IN TRANSLATION   Series 3   Number 2

DIASPORA

Edited by David and Helen Constantine
Cover by Lucy Wilkinson

Contents
Editorial   David and Helen Constantine

Price £11
Available from www.mptmagazine.com

MODERN POETRY IN TRANSLATION   Series 3   Number 3

METAMORPHOSES

Edited by David and Helen Constantine
Cover by Lucy Wilkinson

Contents

Reviews

Antony Wood on Angela Livingstone's *Poems from Chevengur*
Josephine Balmer on Cliff Ashcroft's *Dreaming of Still Water* and
Peter Boyle's Eugenio Montejo
Paschalis Nikolaou on Philip Ramp's Karouzos
Francis Jones on Jan Twardowski (translated by Sarah Lawson and
Malgorzata Koraszweska) and *A Fine Line: New Poetry from Central
and Eastern Europe*

Price £11
Available from www.mptmagazine.com

MODERN POETRY IN TRANSLATION   Series 3   Number 4

BETWEEN THE LANGUAGES

Edited by David and Helen Constantine

Cover by Lucy Wilkinson

Contents

Price £11
Available from www.mptmagazine.com